Online Dispute Resolution

Chandos Internet Series

Chandos' new series of books are aimed at all those individuals interested in the Internet. They have been specially commissioned to provide the reader with an authoritative view of current thinking. If you would like a full listing of current and forthcoming titles, please visit our web site **www.chandospublishing.com** or contact Hannah Grace-Williams on email info@chandospublishing.com or telephone number +44 (0) 1993 848726.

New authors: we are always pleased to receive ideas for new titles; if you would like to write a book for Chandos, please contact Dr Glyn Jones on email gjones@chandospublishing.com or telephone number +44 (0) 1993 848726.

Bulk orders: some organisations buy a number of copies of our books. If you are interested in doing this, we would be pleased to discuss a discount. Please contact Hannah Grace-Williams on email info@chandospublishing.com or telephone number +44 (0) 1993 848726.

Online Dispute Resolution

Technology, management and legal practice from an international perspective

Faye Fangfei Wang

Chandos Publishing
Oxford · England

Chandos Publishing (Oxford) Limited
TBAC Business Centre
Avenue 4
Station Lane
Witney
Oxford OX28 4BN
UK
Tel: +44 (0) 1993 848726 Fax: +44 (0) 1865 884448
Email: info@chandospublishing.com
www.chandospublishing.com

First published in Great Britain in 2009

ISBN:
978 1 84334 519 0 (paperback)
978 1 84334 520 6 (hardback)
1 84334 519 6 (paperback)
1 84334 520 X (hardback)

British Library Cataloguing-in-Publication Data.
A catalogue record for this book is available from the British Library.

Typeset by Domex e-Data Pvt. Ltd.
Printed in the UK and USA.

Contents

List of figures and tables

Figures

Tables

List of abbreviations and acronyms

AAA	American Arbitration Association
ABA	American Bar Association
ACDC	Australian Commercial Disputes Centre Limited
ACR	Association for Conflict Resolution
ADNDRC	Asian Domain Name Dispute Resolution Centre
ADR	alternative dispute resolution
ALI	American Law Institute
B2B	business-to-business
B2C	business-to-consumer
BATNA	best alternative to a negotiated agreement
CAA	Commercial Arbitration Act
CECA	China Electronic Commerce Association
CIETAC	China International Economic and Trade Arbitration Commission
CMAC	China Maritime Arbitration Commission
CNDRP	CNNIC Domain Name Dispute Resolution Policy
CNNIC	China Internet Network Information Center
EC	European Commission
EDI	electronic data interchange
ESIGN Act	Electronic Signatures in Global and National Commerce Act
ETA	Electronic Transactions Act
EU	European Union
EURid	European Registry of Internet Domain Names
GUIDEC	General Usage for International Digitally Ensured Commerce
HKIAC	Hong Kong International Arbitration Centre
IAA	International Arbitration Act 1974
ICANN	Internet Corporation for Assigned Names and Numbers
ICC	International Chamber of Commerce
ICT	information and communication technology

IP	intellectual property
ISP	internet service provider
IT	information technology
NADRAC	National Alternative Dispute Resolution Advisory Council
NCCUSL	The National Conference of Commissioners on Uniform State Laws
ODR	online dispute resolution
OECD	Organisation for Economic Co-operation and Development
RMAB	Recognised Mediation Accreditation Body
S/MIME	Secure Multipurpose Internet Mail Exchange Protocol
SAL	Singapore Academy of Law
SCT	Small Claims Tribunals
SIAC	Singapore International Arbitration Centre
SMC	Singapore Mediation Centre
SME	small and medium-sized entrepreneur
SSL	Secure Sockets Layer
TLS	Transport Layer Security
UCITA	Uniform Computer Information Transactions Act
UDRP	Uniform Domain Name Dispute Resolution Policy
UETA	Uniform Electronic Transactions Act
UNCITRAL	United Nations Commission on International Trade Law
WIPO	World Intellectual Property Organization
WTO	World Trade Organization

Preface

Every year, thousands of multinational companies are emerging in the world, constantly expanding sales and production internationally through the internet. This is largely seen as the key to growing the economy and stimulating globalisation. Transactions in a global market increase the probability of transnational disputes. Moreover parties situated sometimes in different continents are often opposed over small claims.

However, when disputes arise, traditional dispute resolutions become problematic because different countries have different rules for trade and various prohibitive costs of legal action across jurisdictional boundaries. Moreover, for traditional dispute resolutions, the appropriate forum is determined by the place of business or the place of performance. In cyberspace, the localisation factor can be much less obvious as the boundless internet may be accessed from anywhere in the world. Furthermore, when e-disputes only involve a small amount of money, it may not always be cost effective to sue the other party in another county. So how does an e-commerce site resolve disputes? What will be the least costly but more efficient solution?

This book is a guide to help readers understand the challenges of e-commerce; it describes the most up-to-date technology and regulation of online dispute resolution (ODR). It introduces different forms of ODR, against the background of alternative dispute resolution (ADR) developments in the offline environment, examines current technology and the legal status of ODR in the European Union (EU), the US and Asia, and discusses the relationships between the various parties in dispute resolutions, especially the fifth party for the provider of the technology. It further analyses the four most successful examples of dispute resolutions: Michigan cybercourt, ICANN v. WIPO-UDRP, e-Bay v. SquareTrade and AAA v. Cybersettle. Finally, there is a proposal for resolving e-contract disputes via ODR, and a recommendation for a code of conduct in order to regulate the electronic commerce market.

About the author

Dr Faye Fangfei Wang is Lecturer in Law at the University of Bournemouth. In 2007 she was awarded a PhD in Law (Distinction without any correction) at the University of Southampton for her thesis 'Electronic Commercial Transactions: A Comparative Study of International, EU, US and Chinese Law', which gives particular effect to the fields of commercial law, contract law, comparative law and conflicts of law. She was awarded an LLM in Commercial Law (merit with overall distinction) at the University of Aberdeen in 2004 for her dissertation 'Legal Issues Regarding Electronic Signatures and Electronic Authentication: An International Perspective'. She also holds an LLB in International Economic Law in China with a distinction dissertation entitled 'Legal Systems of Electronic Authentication', and she has a Diploma in Computer Science.

Faye (Fei) has worked extensively and internationally in computer, electronic commerce (e-commerce), information technology (IT) and intellectual property (IP) law fields since 2001. She has been a speaker at a number of international legal conferences and published widely on IT and IP law. She teaches LLM students international trade law, in particular on e-commerce and dispute resolutions. Her students benefit from her four years' experience working as a business representative for the China Export Commodities Trade Fair dealing with FOB (Free on Board) and CIF (Cost, Insurance and Freight) international trade contracts with foreign clients.

Her research aims to provide practical solutions to real-world problems in the areas of electronic contracting, electronic signatures (e-signatures), internet jurisdiction, choice of law and online dispute resolution, which are of great value in academia and legislative organisations such as the European Commission (EC) and United Nations Commission on International Trade Law (UNCITRAL), and are of practical value in private business and legal practice.

Background: development of electronic commerce and dispute resolution

Traditionally, when people have disputes, they usually go to courts to resolve them. In the early 1990s, out-of-court dispute resolution mechanisms – alternative dispute resolution (ADR), involving arbitration, mediation and negotiation – were more frequently employed than courts, taking advantage of their speed, flexibility and cost efficiency. In the 21st century, with the emergence of new technologies, electronic communication has been increasingly incorporated into methods of litigation and ADR. This is known as online dispute resolution (ODR). ODR is the equivalent to electronic ADR and cybercourts, moving traditional offline dispute resolution and litigation online. It has been a new, challenging and much researched issue since the mid-1990s. ODR will boost the confidence of doing business online and certainly be more efficient than offline methods, for example, in a case that has an international or cross-border factor but which involves comparatively low financial amounts.

In order to discuss the most updated technology, management and legal perspective of ODR in this book, the first chapter will introduce the background knowledge of e-commerce and discuss how it challenges the traditional legal systems of dealing with international business and dispute resolutions.

1.1 What are electronic commercial transactions?

Computers feature increasingly in our lives. They are used in business to generate increased large profits, which could not easily be achieved by manual means. Computers can also reduce operating costs, increase turnover and improve effective management.[1] The new world has greatly benefited from the speed, compact storage and mathematical analysis of computer technology since the 1980s. It is even more exciting that today computers can be easily connected to the internet and networked with each other, which further enriches our life in many ways and even changes our life pattern. Accordingly, businesses have moved from traditional offline to online platforms. This movement is supported by information and communication technologies (ICTs). Electronic commercial transactions have been at the heart of economic changes for more than a decade.[2] However, it is very difficult to provide a definitive concept of electronic commercial transactions as it can take many different shapes and forms, and thus it can only be understood by first explaining some other relevant concepts.

1.1.1 The internet

The internet is a generic term for connected networks, which can be accessed worldwide. Professor Chris Reed defines the internet as 'an open network which permits communication between parties without the need for both to subscribe to the same closed network'.[3] The internet was initially established in the early 1970s, as the first trans-Atlantic computer networks were linked.[4] Until 1991 the internet was mainly used by the military, governmental and academic sectors.[5] It is only within the last ten years that commerce has increasingly been conducted over the internet, selling goods and providing services electronically.[6]

1.1.2 Electronic commerce: B2B v. B2C

The Organisation for Economic Co-operation and Development (OECD) defines e-commerce as 'all forms of commercial transactions involving both organisations and individuals, which are based upon the electronic processing and transmission of data, including text, sound and visual images. It also refers to the effects that the electronic exchange of commercial information may have on the institutions and process that support and govern commercial activities.'[7]

In the EU, e-commerce is generally deemed to be 'any form of business transaction in which the parties interact electronically rather than by physical exchanges'.[8] Electronic commerce covers mainly two types of activity: 'one is the electronic ordering of tangible goods, delivered physically using traditional channels such as postal services or commercial couriers; and the other is direct e-commerce including the online ordering, payment and delivery of intangible goods and services such as computer software, entertainment content, or information services on a global scale'.[9] In brief, e-commerce is the buying and selling of goods and services using the internet.[10]

In a generic sense, e-commerce is composed of commercial transactions that involve two types of entities, private individuals and commercial entities.[11] From the definitions mentioned above, we can infer a number of factors: primarily, e-commerce presupposes the existence of a business transaction. Additionally, the parties to such a transaction will maintain contact through electronic means rather than traditional ways of communication. Finally, it is designed to create a more efficient business environment.[12] In the author's view, e-commerce is conducted over the internet, using electronic systems to carry on commercial transactions, such as selling goods or providing services.

There are mainly two types of electronic commercial transaction: business-to-business (B2B) transactions and business-to-consumer (B2C) transactions. B2B transactions encompass a complex and fast set of electronic activities between companies.[13] They can be completed by performance against payment or performance against performance.[14] B2C transactions are different, notably because one of the parties acts as a consumer and they involve the purchase of products by individuals outside their trade or profession. Another term for B2C e-commerce is electronic retailing.[15] In short, B2B transactions provide goods or services to other businesses, while B2C transactions sell goods or services to consumers.

1.2 Benefits of e-commerce: its economic and social impacts

A new, universal internet e-economy is emerging without any long-established commercial traditions or geographical borders:[16]

> The year 2006 witnessed the rapid development of e-commerce around the world. E-commerce became a powerhouse for economic globalisation. E-commerce application has become an important factor determining enterprises' international competitiveness. The success of Amazon and e-Bay in the USA and China's Alibaba shows that e-commerce is leading the development of the global

service industry, and affecting the development model of commerce in the future.[17]

In 2006, the OECD also reported that 'the Information and Communication Technology (ICT) industry was expected to grow by 6 per cent in 2006 and, looking ahead, highest growth will be driven by internet-related investments, Linux servers, digital storage, personal digital assistants and new portable consumer products'.[18] ICT trade is also growing even faster than production and sales. With the emergence of new growth economies in Eastern European and non-OECD developing countries, world ICT spending was up 5.6 per cent per year between 2000 and 2005. China was the sixth largest ICT market in 2005 at US$118 billion behind the US, Japan, Germany, UK and France. Although China's total ICT spending is still only about one-tenth that of the US, it is about two and a half times the spending of another newly emerging state, India (US$46 billion). ICT spending in non-OECD countries is still more focused on hardware than on services as the basic physical ICT infrastructure is still being built. After overtaking the US in 2004 as the world's leading ICT exporter, China has continued its strong ICT exports since 2005 and 2006.[19]

In 2006, the overall e-commerce turnover hit US$12.8 trillion, taking up 18 per cent in the global trade of commodities.[20] On 23 January 2007, the China Internet Network Information Center (CNNIC) published the 19th Statistical Survey Report on Internet Development in China.[21] The report shows that by the end of 2006 the number of internet users in China reached 137 million, accounting for 10.5 per cent of China's population.[22] Compared with the same period in 2006, the number of internet users in China has increased by 26 million.[23] At the same time, by the end of 2006, China's online transactions reached a record 1.1 trillion Yuan (around US$125 billion), an increase of 48.6 per cent compared with 2005.[24] In 2007, the e-commerce market in China has still retained its exponential growth with the transaction volume exceeding 1.32 trillion Yuan (around US$150 billion) by August 2007;[25] in particular, B2B generated a total transaction value of 888 million Yuan (US$114 million) during the first quarter of 2007.[26] It is estimated that over 3 million small and medium-sized companies will choose online transactions and their investment in e-commerce will rise by 35 per cent every year to 100 billion Yuan (US$12.49 billion) in 2010.[27] According to the US Department of Commerce, e-commerce transactions in 2003 in the US totalled almost US$1.7 trillion.[28] The vast majority of US e-commerce transactions (93.7 per cent) are B2B rather than B2C.[29] In relation to the EU, according to the statistical survey of the EC, the enterprises' receipts from sales through the internet in the EU took up 4 per cent of the total turnover in 2006, whereas in 2005 there was only 2.7 per cent.[30] Among other statistics, the EU's internet users' growth increased by 170.8 per cent from 2000 to 2007, representing 51.8 per cent of the total EU population and 21.8 per cent of the world usage.[31] It is estimated that starting from zero in 1995, the total e-commerce in the EU was worth €477 billion in 2003, and is expected to reach €2,423 billion by the end of 2007.[32]

E-commerce also presents some additional specific benefits: 'the wide application of e-commerce reduces enterprises' operation and management cost, facilitates the flow of capital, technology, products, services and human resources worldwide, and propels economic globalisation'.[33] Perhaps one of the most obvious features of e-commerce is the speed with which transactions are concluded, for instance, when electronic materials are purchased. A simple downloading of the software in question only takes a few moments. Moreover, due to the internet's global accessibility, a company or legal person offering goods, services or electronic materials by using this medium can reasonably expect to sell products worldwide. Furthermore, once electronic transactions have been concluded, there will be an electronic communication (for example, offer and acceptance or other trading documents), which is easier and more permanent to store than traditional paper documents.

1.3 Technical and legal barriers to e-commerce

1.3.1 The technical context

New information and commutation technologies are growing everyday. Barriers become challenges to lawmakers, because it is crucial to adjust e-commerce regulations to the development of market and technology. Primarily, the lawmakers or law scholars, who are non-computer science experts, may not be familiar with the changing e-transaction technical environment, and will find it difficult to get a genuine insight into the needs of this new and rapidly expanding industry. In addition, new technologies are developed and applied in e-commerce industries in the developed countries while some developing countries like China are still emerging. The technologies employed in some of the developing countries may lag behind and be incompatible with international standards. This raises conflicting issues in relation for instance to security and, therefore, the validity of electronic transactions, especially when involving cross-border deals. This can be affected by slow access speed, insufficient language information on the web, an inability to protect personal privacy or poor internet service providers (ISPs).

1.3.2 E-trust and e-confidence

Trust is central to any commercial transaction. Businesses are often chosen according to whether they can be trusted. The recent Chinese survey 'Lack of Trust Stifles Online Trade' by the China Electronic Commerce Association (CECA) alarmingly discovered that more than a third of Chinese companies with experience in online trading do not trust e-commerce, while an earlier report showed that 71.1 per cent of Chinese internet users who bought and sold online were wary of fraud.[34]

Trust is not a characteristic that is inherent to an e-commerce site, but a judgment made by the end user, based on the personal experience learned from being a customer and from their perception of the particular merchant. Trust can be defined as:

> the subjective assessment of one party that another party will perform a particular transaction according to his or her confident expectations, in an environment characterized by uncertainty.[35]

In e-commerce, there are two basic kinds of trust: identification-based trust and calculus-based trust.[36] The former depends on the existence of a good relationship and empathy between the parties. When the parties care about each other and can understand the other side's perspective, identification-based trust may suffice.[37] With calculus-based trust, individuals do what they promise to do or what is clearly expected of them out of a desire to avoid unpleasant penalties,[38] rather than out of a sense of obligation or empathy. This has also been called deterrence-trust.[39] In brief, trust always entails at least one party being vulnerable to the actions of another, and that party therefore depends on, relies on, or trusts the other party not to exploit that vulnerability.[40] It can be also defined as 'one's willingness to rely on another's actions in a situation involving the risk of opportunism',[41] which can be achieved through 'confidence associated with professional certification, ethics and training'.[42]

With the advent of the internet economy, social trust has become a source of great importance for those concerned with economic expansion. Trust is needed most when risks are perceived to be high, and e-commerce is perceived to be a high risk from all perspectives. This major barrier to participation in e-commerce has been widely discussed in industry publications.[43] People are reluctant to give private information over the internet, because they are concerned about the validity of e-contracts, misuse of credit cards and dispute resolutions. To a considerable extent, businesspeople hesitate to engage in e-market activities because they feel unsafe about:

> i) if and to what extent new partners introduced through the e-market platform at a distance can be trustworthy; ii) if and to what extent the transaction will be executed without problems; iii) if and to what extent, the IT system supporting technically the platform is secure; and iv) if and to what extent, failures in the execution of transactions can be remedied or compensated.[44]

Thus real trust should be established with the intention of creating reliable relationships and enhancing the ability of parties to hold a company accountable for its promises and practices.[45]

Barriers to e-commerce offer opportunities for taking a new look at commercial legal regulations. What makes e-commerce unique and attractive fits uneasily with the traditional legislation. In brief, while the attributes of the internet enable e-commerce, they also hinder its growth for reasons as varied as lack of trust or uncertainty about the regulatory environment.[46] Increased trust can prove beneficial for web businesses. Once users feel more secure, they will visit more websites and conduct more transactions online; overall internet traffic will grow.[47] Building trust and boosting confidence requires legal and technical tools, such as mechanisms for ensuring validity and enforceability of e-contracts, as well as providing security, certification, privacy, redress, users' training[48] and dispute resolutions. These are the key elements for online trust.

1.3.3 Legal obstacles

E-commerce is significant to business, because of its speed and convenience, and the efficiency of the electronic world. As noted, 'e-commerce creates revenue streams, saves costs, and enables businesses to manage their inventory'.[49] Accompanying these benefits, however, are numerous complex and often novel legal issues. Most notably, it is frequently difficult to apply traditional contract laws to the online environment, not least because there are no jurisdictional boundaries in cyberspace. In addition, there are numerous dispute resolution issues that are specific to the online environment. Regardless of the extent to which the 'new e-economy' really does change the way we do business, it will certainly require the world to seek 'new paradigms in many facets of the law'.[50] Companies or legal persons active on the internet may at times be difficult to trace according to traditional criteria – statutory seat, central administration or principal place of business.[51]

Legal certainty is important for transactions carried out electronically. When forming a contract online, there are a number of concerns, such as whether it is enforceable, what the terms are, which court has jurisdiction and whose law applies if there is a breach of contract.[52] The evidential weight of electronic documents must also be considered. For example, will a contract concluded online using an e-signature be admitted in court as evidence and proof of a person's consent to a transaction?[53]

International organisations, the EU and the US have responded to the above concerns by enacting a series of directives or model laws. They have attempted to provide legal frameworks for electronic commercial transactions.

1.4 Regulatory framework of e-commerce

The exponential growth of electronic usage in global commercial transactions has created new challenges to existing laws. Some of the legal solutions still lag behind, because of the unique complexities attached to e-commerce. In order to encourage e-commerce, efforts to reform or establish international commercial laws may be needed to make them suitable to different cultures, economies and policies, practical to enable safe cross-border trading, sufficiently open to the upgrading technology innovations, and manageable to build up e-trust and e-confidence.

1.4.1 Global regimes

The UN Convention on the Use of Electronic Communications in International Contracts[54] (hereafter 'the UN Convention') was adopted by the General Assembly on 23 November 2005. The primary purpose of the UN Convention is 'to facilitate international trade by removing possible legal obstacles or uncertainty concerning the use of electronic communications in connection with the formation or performance of contracts concluded between parties located in different countries'.[55] It aims to 'enhance legal certainty and commercial predictability' in international electronic contracts. It addresses issues such as legal recognition of electronic communication, the location of parties, the time and place of dispatch and receipt of electronic communication, use of automated message systems for contract formation, availability of contract terms and errors in electronic communications.[56] The UN Convention is also intended to be as technologically neutral as possible, in order to cover electronic communications in multiple forms in relation to existing or contemplated contracts exchanged between parties.[57] It intends to stimulate the progress to harmonise national laws, which will at least reduce legal uncertainty in transnational business transactions.

The UNCITRAL Model Law on Electronic Commerce[58] (hereafter 'the Model Law on E-Commerce') was adopted by UNCITRAL on 12 June 1996. Generally, as a minimalist approach, the primary motivation is to remove existing legal obstacles to the recognition and enforceability of e-signatures and records. It does not address specific techniques, and therefore it intends to be technology-neutral. This minimalist approach focuses on verifying the intent of the signing party rather than developing particularised forms and guidelines.[59] It is supposed to help states enhance their legislation on electronic communications and to serve as a reference aid for the interpretation of existing international conventions and other instruments in order to avoid impediments to e-commerce.[60] The Model Law on E-Commerce deals generally with the use of modern means of electronic communications and storage of information,[61] the formation and validity of electronic contracts,[62] the legal recognition of data messages[63] and the carriage of goods.[64]

Electronic signature and authentication is an encryption technology, which is employed in electronic commercial transactions to ensure online business security. However, there is a need to promulgate model laws and national regulations to remove the legal uncertainty of the identity recognition of online parties and the validity of their conducts. This led the UN Commission on International Trade Law to declare that 'the risk that diverging legislative approaches be taken in various countries with respect to e-signatures calls for uniform legislative provisions to establish the basic rules of what is inherently an international phenomenon, where legal harmony as well as technical interoperability is a desirable objective'.[65]

The UNCITRAL Model Law on Electronic Signatures[66] (hereafter 'the Model Law on E-Signatures') was adopted by UNCITRAL on 5 July 2001. It follows a technology-neutral approach, which avoids favouring the use of any specific technical product.[67] This approach achieves legal neutrality by granting minimum recognition to most authentication technologies, while at the same time incorporating provisions for an authentication technology of choice.[68] It gives a developed legal framework for certificate service provision within an international operative public key infrastructure and promotes the progressive harmonisation and unification of measures and policies on e-signature issues.

The International Chamber of Commerce (ICC) was founded in 1919 with an overriding aim that remains unchanged: to serve world business by promoting trade and investment, open markets for goods and services, and the free flow of capital.[69] The ICC has become the world's largest business organisation dedicated to business self-regulation, with over 8,000 member companies and associations in more than 130 countries. It sets voluntary rules that companies from all parts of the world apply to millions of transactions every year. It also contributes to international and regional initiatives on electronic contracting,[70] like for instance the General Usage for International Digitally Ensured Commerce (GUIDEC), ICC e-Terms 2004 and the ICC Guide to Electronic Contracting. The GUIDEC has built on the work of UNCITRAL Model Law on E-Commerce and the American Bar Association's (ABA's) Digital Signature Guidelines. It attempts to create a general framework for the use of digital signatures in international commercial transactions. It mainly deals with digital signatures and the role of registration and certification authorities in e-commerce. Moreover, the ICC e-Terms 2004 are designed to enhance the legal certainty of contract made by electronic means, providing parties with two short articles, easy to incorporate into contracts, which expressly state that both parties agree to be bound by an electronic contract.[71] The e-terms can be used for any contract for the sale or other arrangement of goods or services. The ICC e-Terms 2004 aim to facilitate the procedures and the use of electronic means in concluding a contract without interfering with the subject matter of the contract and any other agreed terms between parties. The ICC e-Terms 2004 can be applied in any type of electronic contracting, through a website, by e-mail or by electronic data interchange (EDI). They are seen as a logical extension of the ICC's array of rules, model contract clauses and guidelines that feature daily in countless paper-based international business transactions.[72] Furthermore, the ICC Guide to Electronic Contracting (hereafter 'the Guide') answered the questions, for instance, how to apply ICC e-Terms 2004; what is the legal validity of ICC e-Terms 2004; what are the limits of ICC e-Terms 2004; who contracts on your behalf; with whom are you contracting; how to construct an electronic contract; what are technical specifications; how to protect confidentiality; and how to cope with technical breakdown and risk management. The Guide provides a useful explanatory supplement to the ICC e-Terms

(2004); however, it would have been advisable to split it into subsections to make it clearer for the use of e-terms.

At the same time, other international organisations such as the OECD and the World Trade Organization (WTO) also regulate e-commerce taking into account cultural, economic and political differences. The OECD 'has permitted a broad-based policy reflection on the establishment of an adequate infrastructure, as well as the elements that would provide a favourable environment for electronic commerce and the digital economy',[73] whereas the WTO takes into account the economic, financial and development needs of developing countries.

1.4.2 Other regimes

1.4.2.1 The European Union

Electronic commerce is a product from the IT revolution developed within the global marketplace, including the EU. With these growing numbers in mind, up-to-date legislation is imperative in order to meet the expanding needs of commercial transactions over the internet. In order to keep pace with market developments, the EU has already created an extensive legal framework addressing various issues on 'information society services' and, most notably, e-commerce. These include the directive 'Certain Legal Aspects of Information Society Services, in Particular Electronic Commerce in the Internal Market', 2000/31/EC, 8 June 2000 (hereafter 'the E-Commerce Directive'), and the directive 'A Community Framework for Electronic Signatures' 1993/93/EC, 13 December 1999 (hereafter 'the E-Signatures Directive').

In relation to the latter, Frits Bolkestein, the former Internal Market Commissioner, said that 'the EC Directive is helping e-commerce to take off in the Internal Market by ensuring that Europe's e-commerce entrepreneurs can take full advantage of a domestic market of more than 370 million consumers'.[74] Among the two related directives, the E-Commerce Directive[75] plays an important role in regulating electronic transactions in the internal market between member states. In order to enhance its efficiency, this directive lays down a clear and general framework to cover certain legal aspects of e-commerce in the internal market by creating a legal framework to ensure the free movement of information society services between member states. It creates various rules including: a transparency obligation on operators in commercial communications;[76] electronic contracts; limitations of liability of intermediary service providers; and provisions for online dispute settlement. However, the E-Signatures Directive[77] is a far more detailed directive and sets out a framework for the recognition of e-signatures and certification service requirements for member states.[78] Article 1 specifies that the aim of the directive is to establish a legal framework for e-signatures and certain certification services. It facilitates the use and legal recognition of e-signatures, while ensuring the proper functioning of the internal market.[79] This should lead to the E-Signatures Directive promoting cross-border e-commerce within the EU by encouraging electronic contracts.[80] However, the directive does not cover 'aspects related to the conclusion and validity of contracts', which is dealt with in the E-Commerce Directive.[81] Also excluded are 'legal obligations where there are requirements as regards form prescribed by national or Community Law' and, finally, the directive is not meant to 'affect rules and limits, contained in national or Community law, governing the use of documents'.[82]

1.4.2.2 The United States

The US is a free-market, capitalist economy. This has become even more apparent as the US attempts, through its role as the world's economic hegemony, to spread political and economic deregulation via treaties (both bilateral and multilateral), and its role in, and arguably control over, international organisations such as the UN or the WTO. As a free-market economy, the US in principle subscribes to a hands-off, minimalist approach to the regulation of commerce.[83] However, the need for a coherent set of rules that would promote certainty, predictability and security gave rise to action by US authorities at both state and federal level. Proposed and enacted legislation dealing with electronic contracting capabilities are heavily influenced by the UNCITRAL Model Law on E-Commerce and, in general tend to reflect the functional equivalent method to writing requirements.[84] According to Bill Clinton's Framework for Global Electronic Commerce, there are five principles that the US and other nations, should adhere to in attempting to regulate e-commerce:

> (1) The private sector should lead; (2) Governments should avoid undue restrictions on electronic commerce; (3) Where governmental involvement is needed, its aim should be to support and enforce a predictable, minimalist, consistent, and simple legal environment for commerce; (4) Governments should recognize the unique qualities of the internet; and (5) Electronic Commerce over the internet should be facilitated on a global basis.[85]

Each individual state in the US has considered the ramifications of e-commerce and e-signatures and has either passed or is introducing e-signature legislation. As each state has a different law on e-signatures, some groups and organisations have attempted to standardise and unify the various laws into a uniform law. The National Conference of Commissioners on Uniform State Laws (NCCUSL) and the American Law Institute (ALI) have promulgated separate state uniform laws addressing e-signatures, the Uniform Computer Information Transactions Act (UCITA) and the Uniform Electronic Transactions Act (UETA).[86]

The UCITA, initially originated from a proposal for a new Uniform Commercial Code Article 2 and approved as a legislative model by the NCCUSL on 29 July 1999, has only been signed and enacted by two states – Maryland and Virginia.[87] The UCITA is a model 'uniform commercial code' for software licences and other computer information transactions. It addresses issues such as digital signatures, electronic records and electronic agents. The UCITA adopts the accepted and familiar principles of contract law. This act provides a set of comprehensive rules for licensing computer information, whether computer software or other clearly identified forms of computer information.[88]

It also governs access contracts to sites containing computer information, whether online or offline. The UCITA also applies to storage devices, such as disks and CDs that exist only to hold computer information. Other kinds of goods, which contain computer information as a material part of the subject matter of a transaction, may also be made subject to the UCITA by express reference in a contract. Otherwise, other laws will apply, such as the law of sales or leases for most transactions. The UCITA does not govern contracts, even though they may be licensing contracts, for the traditional distribution of movies, books, periodicals, newspapers or the like.[89] It is apparent that the UCITA is intended to operate in a similar fashion to the UNCITRAL Model Law on E-Commerce through reliance on functional equivalency and avoiding specific technological requirements.[90]

The UETA, promulgated in July 1999, like the UCITA, is a model code, which has been adopted by 48 states and the District of Columbia.[91] It differs from the UCITA in that it is addressed to electronic transactions generally. The aim of the NCCUSL in fashioning the UETA was to provide states with a set of uniform rules governing e-commerce transactions.[92]

The primary objective of the UETA is to provide electronic transactions with the same legal effect as paper transactions without changing any applicable substantive laws. Under the UETA, parties are free to choose a contract electronically or through traditional means. Furthermore, parties may agree to use only part of the provisions of the UETA, even if business will be transacted by electronic means. Furthermore, the UETA differs from the UCITA in that the former governs all electronic transactions, whereas the latter does not deal directly with the substantive issues involved with electronic contracts.[93]

The Electronic Signatures in Global and National Commerce Act (ESIGN Act) was signed by President Clinton on 30 June 2000 and most of its provisions became effective on 1 October 2000. The ESIGN Act was enacted, in part, to promote consistency and certainty regarding the use of e-signatures in the US.[94] The ESIGN Act, like the UCITA, adopts a technology-neutral approach, different from the two-tier approach of the UETA. This act regulates any transactions in interstate and foreign commerce. It provides a framework that is intended to facilitate transactions in electronic form or includes an e-signature, which includes several key provisions concerning, for example, its scope, validity requirements for e-signatures, electronic contracts and electronic records or retention requirements for electronic contracts and goods.

1.4.2.3 Asia: Singapore and China

In Singapore, the Electronic Transactions Act[95] (ETA) was adopted on 10 July 1988 in order to 'facilitate electronic communications and promote public confidence in the integrity and reliability of electronic records and electronic commerce, and foster the development of electronic commerce through the use of e-signatures to lend authenticity and integrity to correspondence in any electronic medium'.[96] The Singapore ETA is based largely on the provisions of the UNCITRAL Model Law on E-Commerce, dealing extensively with electronic contracts and e-signatures.

Unlike Singapore, China did not have any state law regulating e-commerce until 2005. The Standing Committee of the 10th National People's Congress passed the Law of the People's Republic of China on Electronic Signatures (Chinese Electronic Signatures Law) on 28 August 2004,[97] which entered into effect on 1 April 2005, providing a legal basis for electronic transactions. This implementation of the e-commerce law dramatically promotes the development of the Chinese e-business market, as before the legal framework and the necessary infrastructure for the use of digital signatures was established, electronic contracting was not widely used in business transactions in China.

The Chinese Electronic Signatures Law regulates the act of electronic signature, establishing the legal effect of e-signature, and maintaining the lawful rights and interests of the relevant parties concerned.[98] It applies to parties who may stipulate their intention to use or not to use e-signature or data message in the contract or other documents and civil documentations. Any document using e-signatures or data messages has the same legal effect as handwritten documents. The Chinese Electronic Signatures Law leaves the parties to decide whether or not to use e-signatures and messages in its provisions. However, certain types of agreements such as those relating to personal relations, the transfer of real estate rights and interests, and public utility services cannot use electronic means as prescribed by laws and administrative regulations, and have to apply to continue to use traditional formal signatures – in writing.[99]

1.4.2.4 Australia

The Australian Government has adopted a function equivalent and technology neutral regulatory approach to facilitate the development of e-commerce by removing legal impediments. The Electronic Transactions Act 1999 of the Commonwealth[100] provides rules on legal recognition of electronic communications, the time and place of dispatch and receipt of messages, and the retention of electronic records. Similar to Singapore, the legislation is based on the UNCITRAL Model Law on E-Commerce recommended by its Electronic Commerce Expert Group. The Uniform Electronic Transactions Bill 2000,[101] closely modelled on the Electronic Transactions Act 1999, is endorsed by the state and territory governments in cooperation with the Commonwealth government.[102] In the author's view, the relationship between the Act and the Bill in Australia is similar to the relationship between the EC Directive and the (UK) Regulation in the EU.

According to the above discussion of e-commerce legislation in various jurisdictions, although there are different rules in between, there is one provision that is definitely in common at both international and national levels, that is, contracts can be formed by electronic means of communication. Thus, electronic contracts are equivalent to paper-based contracts. In the era of information technology, any computer, anywhere in the world, connected to the internet can access a website. Businesses, through the use of the internet, can enter into electronic contracts with other businesses located in different countries. The potential for cross-border disputes in web contracts is, obviously, much greater than in a paper-based environment where many commercial contracts are domestic in nature. Businesses fear that the determination of internet jurisdiction could be uncertain because, unlike paper-based contracts, online contracting is not executed in one particular place. Therefore, nations want to be able to ensure the protection of local businesses. Given the nature of the internet, in particular the distance between buyer and seller, as well as the prohibitive cost of legal action across jurisdictional boundaries, how does an e-commerce site resolve disputes? What will be the least costly but more efficient solution?

1.5 Dispute resolution

Traditional litigation is very complicated to apply to international business disputes because it is very difficult to determine which court will hear the case and whose law will apply. It will be even more complicated if those international business disputes involve electronic communication or electronic transactions, as the determination of place of business or place of performance over the internet is different from the traditional jurisdiction rules. Currently, there are no specific rules in the model laws and conventions dealing with internet jurisdiction. The UNCITRAL Model Law on E-Commerce and the UN Convention on the Use of Electronic Communications in International Contracts do not contain any jurisdiction provisions.

Although parties may agree in advance a choice of court and choice of law clause, litigation through the court system can still be a time-consuming process because of all the formalities that must be followed in any court-based process of litigation. Moreover, it is often inflexible as it is based on a formal model that is heavily governed by rules and procedures. It can also be adversarial, which might poison or destroy a more valuable long-term business relationship between the parties over a minor business problem.[103]

As a result, some parties today may choose a more flexible and friendly forum – ADR as a way of handling difficulties. ADR can be chosen by agreement at any time, even after a dispute has arisen. It mainly includes three methods of dispute settlement:

- *Negotiation*? Persons seek to resolve a disagreement or plan a transaction through discussion.[104] It can be used in all manner of disputes and transactions.
- *Mediation*? Mediation is an informal process in which an impartial third party helps others resolve a dispute or plan a transaction but it does not impose a solution.[105]
- *Arbitration*? In arbitration, the parties agree to submit their dispute to a neutral party whom they have selected to make a decision.[106]

Furthermore, some mixed processes are also recommended as means of dispute settlement, such as mediation-arbitration; 'med-arb' begins as mediation. If the parties do not reach an agreement, they proceed to arbitration.[107]

In recent years, as transactions in a global market mean an increased probability of transnational disputes, parties situated sometimes in different continents are opposed over small claims. Moreover, most of the evidence is stored in electronic forms or files. Courts or traditional out-of-court dispute resolution mechanisms cannot reasonably resolve such conflicts. As a consequence, a new tool for dispute resolution has appeared, which is more efficient, more cost effective and more flexible than traditional approaches: this is online dispute resolution (ODR).[108] ODR is a dispute resolution that takes advantage of the internet, a resource that extends what we can do, where we can do it, and when we can do it.[109] It is a new solution to build trust in electronic commercial transactions.

As international dispute resolution is a vast topic, this book will only focus on disputes involving an international business context. The objectives of this book are to introduce different forms of ODR, against the background of ADR developments in the offline environment, and to examine current technology, management and the legislative frameworks of ODR in the EU, the US, China, Singapore, Australia and international organisations in general. It then discusses the relations between the various parties in dispute resolutions, especially the fifth party for the provider of the technology. It further analyses four successful experiences of Michigan Cybercourt, the existing ODR mechanisms developed by e-Bay and its authorised ODR provider 'SquareTrade', World Intellectual Property Organization (WIPO) and the Internet Corporation for Assigned Names and Numbers (ICANN) Uniform Domain Name Dispute Resolution Policy (UDRP), as well as AAA and Cybersettle. This will enable us to examine what might cause a lack of trust in ODR and to determine how to build up e-confidence, and to make recommendations of core principles and model codes of conduct on ODR. Finally, we make a proposal for resolving e-contract disputes via ODR.

One of the key features of this book is that it provides in-depth research into the barriers to online dispute resolutions and answers them by finding the solutions. There are two main questions about electronic dispute settlement:

- How can disputes be resolved online?
- How can the decisions of online dispute resolution be enforced?

With regard to the first question, this book aims to clarify the mechanism of ODR referring to electronic contracting disputes. The three successful examples examined in this book will explain that the linking of ODR service providers and primary market makers as well as the self-enforcement mechanism of resolution outcomes are key credentials to their success. The book then highlights how important information processing is in any dispute resolution process for the dispute resolution community. Appropriate software acts as a fourth party, which can help parties negotiate without the help of a third party or help a third party work with the parties. Although ODR's obvious role is to settle disputes and bring some satisfactions to users, its second role is to send users a message that a particular website is safe to participate in because if a problem arises a process is in place to resolve it. Any tool that contributes to a user's calculation of risk and assessment of trust is important because all the conveniences and cost savings that a network makes possible are worthless if the systems are not actually used. Thus they are being built through collaboration and the creative contributions of users. The six core principles of the conduct of ODR – accountability, confidentiality, accessibility, credibility, security and enforceability – will also be evaluated in this book.

The second question is concerned with the enforceability of the decisions of ODR. Enforceability, one of the six core principles of the conduct of ODR, is essential, since its success will encourage electronic traders or businesses to use ODR to resolve their disputes. The outcomes of online mediation and negotiation should be able to convert into settlement agreements, while the decisions of online arbitration should constitute arbitral awards. Otherwise, the ODR service providers should have their self-enforcement or self-execution mechanisms to enforce contractual dispute settlements.

Based on the above main focuses, the forthcoming chapters will discuss the most updated issues related to ODR technology, management and legal practice from an international perspective and recommend a proposal for the conduct of ODR.

Notes

1. Mawrey and Salmon (1988), pp. 1–3.
2. OECD (2007).
3. Reed and Angel (2007), p. 198.
4. Terrett and Monaghan (2000), p. 2.

5. Lloyd (2004), p. 40.
6. Ibid., p. 42.
7. OECD (1997b).
8. Commission of the European Union (1997).
9. Ibid.
10. EC (2005).
11. Reed and Angel (2007), p. 198.
12. Rosner (2004), p. 483.
13. Vittet-Philippe (2000), p. 1.
14. Rosner (2004), p. 483. An example of performance against performance is when one party supplies statistical data in exchange for the results of market research.
15. Rosner (2004), p. 483.
16. Mills (2004), p. 443.
17. CCID Consulting (2007b).
18. OECD (2006).
19. Ibid.
20. CCID Consulting (2007b).
21. CNNIC (2007b).
22. CNNIC (2007a, 2007b).
23. CNNIC (2007b).
24. CCID Consulting (2007a).
25. CMIC (2007b).
26. CMIC (2007a).
27. Xinhua News Agency (2006).
28. US Dept of Commerce (2005); Xinhua News Agency (2006).
29. US Dept of Commerce (2005); Xinhua News Agency (2006).
30. EUROSTAT (2007).
31. Internet World Stats (2007). According to the 2005 statistics, the number of internet users increased by 143.5% between 2000 and 2005. In 2005 49.3% of the EU population were internet users.
32. EITO (n.d.).
33. CCID Consulting (2007b).
34. *China Daily* (2006).
35. Ba and Pavlou (2002), pp. 243, 245.
36. Raines (2006), pp. 359, 364.
37. Ibid.
38. Lewicki and Wiethoff (2000); cited from Raines (2006), pp. 359, 364.
39. Raines (2006), pp. 359, 364.
40. Hosmer (1995), pp. 379, 381–2.
41. Williams (2001), pp. 377, 378.
42. Ibid.
43. Mutz (2005), pp. 393, 398.
44. EC (2006), p. 18.
45. Fort and Liu (2002), pp. 1545, 1552–3.
46. OECD (1997a).
47. Goldman (2006), pp. 353, 369.
48. OECD (1997a).

49. Schulze and Baumgartner (2001).
50. Mills (2004), p. 431.
51. Rosner (2004), p. 491.
52. Bainbridge (2008), p. 355.
53. Ibid., p. 357.
54. UN General Assembly (2005).
55. UNCITRAL (2007).
56. See http://www.uncitral.org/uncitral/en/uncitral_texts/electronic_commerce/2005Convention.html (accessed 7 April 2007).
57. Connolly and Ravindra (2005).
58. UNCITRAL Model Law on Electronic Commerce.
59. Moreno (2001).
60. Glatt (1998), p. 57.
61. See http://www.uncitral.org/uncitral/en/uncitral_texts/electronic_commerce/1996Model.html (accessed 7 April 2007).
62. The UNCITRAL Model Law on Electronic Commerce, Article 11.
63. Ibid., Articles 6–8.
64. Ibid., Article 16.
65. UNCITRAL Model Law on Electronic Signatures with Guide to Enactment 2001.
66. UNCITRAL Model Law on Electronic Signatures of the UN Commission on International Trade Law, Agenda Item 16, A/RES/56/80, 24 January 2002.
67. See http://www.uncitral.org/uncitral/en/uncitral_texts/electronic_commerce/2001Model_signatures.html (accessed 7 April 2007).
68. Moreno (2001).
69. 'What is ICC?', available at http://www.iccwbo.org/id93/index.html (accessed 11 July 2008).
70. Astrup (2003).
71. See http://www.iccwbo.org (accessed 9 March 2005).
72. ICC (2003a).
73. OECD (2001).
74. EC (2003).
75. Directive 2000/31/EC (the E-Commerce Directive).
76. Bogle and Mitchell (2000).
77. Directive 1999/93/EC (the E-Signatures Directive).
78. Thurlow (2001).
79. Ibid.
80. Copeland (2000).
81. Lodder (2000).
82. Article 1 of the EC Directive on Electronic Signatures.
83. Pappas (2002), pp. 325, 327.
84. Boss (1998), pp. 1931, 1933.
85. Clinton and Gore (1997).
86. Lupton (1999).
87. ALA (2006).
88. For a summary of the UCITA see http://www.nccusl.org/nccusl/ucita/UCITA_Summary.pdf (accessed 7 September).

89. Uniform Law Commissioners (n.d.).
90. Thurlow (2001).
91. As of October 2004, 48 states and the District of Columbia had enacted UETA; see http://www.nccusl.org/nccusl/newsletters/ULC/ULCbull_Oct04_print.pdf (accessed 18 November 2004).
92. See summary of the UETA at http://www.nccusl.org/Update/uniformact_summaries/uniformacts-s-ueta.asp (accessed 7 September 2007).
93. Nimmer (2001b).
94. Gidari and Morgan (2000).
95. Singapore Electronic Transactions Act 1998, available at Singapore Statutes Online, http://statutes.agc.gov.sg/non_version/cgi-bin/cgi_retrieve.pl?actno=REVED-88&doctitle=ELECTRONIC%20TRANSACTIONS%20ACT%0A&date=latest&method=part&sl=1 (accessed 19 May 2008).
96. Singapore Electronic Transactions Act 1998, Article 3.
97. Law of the People's Republic of China on Electronic Signatures (hereafter 'Chinese Electronic Signatures Law'), PRCLEG 3691, 2004, available at http://www.transasialawyers.com/translation/legis_03_e.pdf (accessed 7 September 2007).
98. Chinese Electronic Signatures Law, Article 1.
99. Ibid., Article 3.
100. Australia Electronic Transactions Act, No. 162, 1999, available at http://scaleplus.law.gov.au/html/comact/10/6074/pdf/162of99.pdf (accessed 19 May 2008).
101. Electronic Transactions Bill 2000, available at http://www.legislation.qld.gov.au/Bills/49PDF/2000/ElectronicTransQldB00Exp.pdf [Queensland] and http://www.parliament.nsw.gov.au/prod/parlment/nswbills.nsf/7bd7da67ee5a02c5ca256e67000c8755/eb9de97c8c0e249cca2568b7001edfbf/$FILE/b99-006-p03.pdf [New South Wales] (accessed 19 May 2008).
102. Australian Department – the Attorney-General's Department, available at http://www.ag.gov.au/www/agd/agd.nsf/Page/e-commerce_Frequentlyaskedquestions (accessed 19 May 2008).
103. Chow and Schoenbaum (2005), pp. 661–2.
104. Riskin and Westbrook (1998), p. 4.
105. Ibid., p. 4.
106. Ibid., p. 3.
107. Ibid., p. 5.
108. Bonnet et al. (2004), see generally.
109. Katsh and Rifkin (2001), p. 10.

2

The context of ODR

2.1 Overview of ODR

ODR is usually known as any of online ADR, e-ADR, iADR, virtual ADR and cyber ADR. It was technologically developed in the US and Canada, and it is still used mainly in the US.[1] In the mid-1990s ODR started with four venues: the Virtual Magistrate at Villanova University, the Online Ombuds Office at the University of Massachusetts, the Online Mediation Project at the University of Maryland, and the CyberTribunal Project at the University of Montreal, Canada.[2] Whereas early ODR endeavours were non-profit venues sponsored by universities and foundations, today's ODR venues are mainly profit commercial ventures providing services for both B2B and B2C online transactions.[3] A study conducted in 2004 revealed the existence of 115 ODR sites, 82 of which were still operational, while 28 new sites or services launched between 2003 and 2004.[4] ODR uses the internet as a more efficient medium for parties to resolve both contractual disputes, such as B2B and B2C transactions, and non-contractual disputes, such as those about copyright, data protection, the right of free expression, competition law and domain names.

For e-commerce entrepreneurs, ODR is attractive as it is something that can be incorporated into their new ventures as part of an overall strategy to build trust among users.[5] Reliable dispute resolution systems bolster their confidence in e-commerce and stimulate transaction volume. Developing trust and confidence worldwide is highly culture-related, while offering a universal dispute resolution mechanism that would take charge of the problem whenever and wherever it emerges is challenging, because when personal and cultural variations happen, different patterns of disputers' complaining behaviours occur. There is a growing need to establish a set of rules that suits both same- and cross-cultural disputers.

In order to facilitate a change in paradigm from resolving e-contract disputes using mouse-to-mouse ODR, rather than traditional face-to-face dispute resolutions, online ADR rules or regulations are needed. The author believes that ODR, like all of e-commerce, needs to have mechanisms to build trust in dealings about goods or services. In thinking about how to build up a certain level of e-confidence, we should ask ourselves the following questions:

1. What constitutes lack of trust?
2. What information must ODR providers keep confidential? From that perspective, what security measures are taken to protect the confidentiality and will the principle of confidentiality conflict with transparency?
3. If disputers are unsatisfied with the ODR providers, where can they complain? Or if ODR providers breach service agreements, which court will have jurisdiction? And what will be the online jury proceedings?
4. How can the enforcement problem of online arbitration awards be resolved?

So what induces a lack of trust in ODR? In face-to-face dispute resolution, trust is established during the resolution sessions. In the offline world, when we walk into a shop, a bank or another place that expects us to enter into a relationship requiring some degree of trust, we should be impressed by how hard these places try to inspire trust in us. Expensive buildings and furniture, for instance, are considered signs of credibility.

In the online environment, obviously these signs are not present. Before disputing parties choose an ODR mechanism, they will worry about lack of familiarity of the ODR system, theft of identity and credit card information, lack of transparent and effective technology solutions, and lack of controls when ODR providers do not keep their service promise.

2.2 Understanding ODR

2.2.1 Descriptions of ODR: e-ADR and cybercourts

ADR is a private dispute resolution. The basic forms of ADR are arbitration, mediation and negotiation. Arbitration is an adversarial procedure in which an independent third party decides the case, while mediation and negotiation are consensual procedures in which the disputants aim to reach agreement, either on their own or assisted by a third party called the mediator or conciliator. With the development of technology, ODR designated cyberspace as a location for dispute resolution, moving ADR from a physical to a virtual place. That is, ODR services are the online transposition of the methods developed in the ADR movement. However, ODR not only employs the ADR processes in the online environment but also enhances these processes in offline environments.[6]

The ABA Task Force on E-Commerce and ADR provides a generic definition of ODR:

> ODR is a broad term that encompasses many forms of ADR and court proceedings that incorporate the use of the internet, websites, e-mail communications, streaming media and other information technology as part of the dispute resolution process. Parties may never meet face to face when participating in ODR. Rather, they might communicate solely online.[7]

The Australia National Alternative Dispute Resolution Advisory Council (NADRAC) defines ODR as 'processes where a substantial part, or all, of the communication in the dispute resolution process takes place electronically, especially via e-mail'.[8] Edwards and Wilson divide ODR into 'hard' ODR, referring to 'procedures intending directly to resolve conflicts' such as traditional ADR, and 'soft' ODR, relating to 'procedures seeking to prevent disputes' such as e-Bay's feedback system for reputation ranking.[9] In the author's opinion, ODR should be defined as online procedures to resolve disputes or conflicts covering e-ADR and cybercourts. The e-Bay feedback system, on the other hand, should merely be regarded as a trust or reputation-ranking scheme, which can be used as a supplement for ODR to build trust in e-transactions.

When talking about ODR, the less familiar method of dispute resolution is 'cybercourts', also known as virtual courts, e-courts or cyber tribunals. They now exist for instance in Michigan, Ohio, Puerto Rico, Australia and the UK. Cybercourts permit the presentation of evidence online and, with the help of video conferencing, allow the court to hold informational hearings and receive witness testimony online if the need arises.[10]

It is necessary to point out that ODR is not meant to replace or be a substitute for face-to-face settings when they can be part of the process.[11] In the arena of online dispute resolutions, who can take control? Thomas Schulz argues that governments must exert control because they are the most trusted entity in the field of dispute resolution.[12] Colin Rule agrees that:

> to a large extent, government is the ideal host for dispute resolution, because government has a strong incentive to resolve disputes to keep society functioning smoothly, Government is also a good host for dispute resolution because it usually has no vested interest in the outcome of most of the matters it is in charge of deciding.[13]

In the author's opinion, although there are advantages if government controls ODR, there are also disadvantages, because if government is in charge of ODR, which government will take control: that of the EU, US or Asia? Whose ruling will be more favourable when international disputants are involved? Whose government will gain trust from global users?

International organisations such as UNCITRAL, OECD, ICC, WIPO and WTO, as well as some other globally well-known organisations such as ABA, should exert control of ODR to overcome the above problems for the following reasons:

- International organisations have a worldwide reputation and image.
- They are identical to governments, which can make use of their 'symbolic capital'.[14] OECD, ICC, WIPO or WTO can operate ODR or accredit ODR providers as brands through symbolic capital, which instils trust in dispute resolution.
- Similar to governments, the intervention of international organisations does not aim to be economically profitable and they have funding from grants, private sectors or governments.
- International organisations can regulate ODR uniformly, which will be an advantage in cross-border dispute settlements. At the same time, these self-regulations can provide a base for establishing an international model law in ODR in the future.

2.2.2 Characteristics of ODR

2.2.2.1 ADR v. litigation

Litigation tends to end with one party being the winner and the other the loser.[15] If revenge or destroying the other party is a goal, courts and trials will continue to be attractive.[16] ADR, however, is viewed as an opportunity for better or more appropriate resolutions than can be provided in court.[17] The ideal of ADR is a win–win solution: an outcome that the parties are satisfied with and which might even allow them to work together in the future.[18]

Compared with litigation, ADR has the following advantages:

- *Greater speed*: Court proceedings may take a long time. It may take months, sometimes years, before a case can be brought before a court. A hearing is generally more quickly arranged in mediation and often in arbitration proceedings. If the arbitrators make it clear to the parties that they understand the essence of the dispute, the parties don't need to repeat their arguments but can direct their attention specifically to the points that are still unclear to the arbitrators, thus saving time and money.
- *Lower costs*: ADR generally costs less than litigation. In ADR, the issue of costs may be dealt with in the settlement agreement and is therefore totally within the control of the parties. When cases are resolved earlier through ADR, the parties may save some of the money they would have spent on attorney fees, court costs and expert fees. However, ADR is not always cheap, and can be as expensive as court action, particularly because arbitrator or mediators have to be paid for their services.
- *An informal settlement with more flexibility in outcomes*: The ADR proceedings are less formal than court proceedings. The procedural rules are often established in agreement between the parties. Arbitrators and lawyers do not wear gowns. Parties' counsel do not plead from the bench like barristers in court; on the contrary, arbitrators, lawyers and parties often sit around one big conference table. However, some arbitrators insist on a degree of formality which replicates court procedures.
- *Settlement by experts*: The courts usually have sufficient general expertise to settle commercial disputes. However, some disputes require extensive technical knowledge. It is impossible for a judge who has to adjudicate all kinds of disputes to be an all-round technical expert. The judge may of course appoint an expert, though the intervention of the expert takes time and adds to the costs. It can therefore be better to give the expert the task of adjudicating the dispute directly – appoint an arbitrator sufficiently familiar with the technical and commercial background of the dispute so that no further expert is needed.
- *Privacy and confidentiality*: Court proceedings are public. In principle, arbitration is not public. The proceedings of ADR are entirely confidential.

- *International settlement with fewer jurisdictional problems*: ADR is often the better way to settle an international commercial dispute. From a practical perspective, going to court is a complicated method of conflict resolution in the global environment of the internet. If a dispute arises between you and an international business partner or customer, they may file civil lawsuits against you in a foreign court located in their home state or country.[19] Also, each of the parties may refuse to submit to the jurisdiction of a court in the country of the other party, for fear of being at a disadvantage. In addition, e-businesses may find themselves dealing with different courts that are applying different laws to the same dispute, resulting in enormous costs and lost time and productivity.[20] That said, in recent years there have been proceedings, e.g. by jurisdictional challenges or by commencing judicial proceedings, and much satellite litigation has resulted.
- *A less adversarial, more effective process with better results*: Mediation generally enjoys an 80–85 per cent success rate.[21] Moreover, the resolution is created by the parties, so it should be deemed to work better between them.
- *Enforceability*: An arbitration award is generally easier to enforce abroad than a court decision, because existing international treaties favour arbitration over national courts.[22] However, the basis for arbitration is an agreement between parties; the award does not bind third parties. Requests for third party intervention or for consolidation of related arbitration proceedings can only be entertained if all parties agreed to multi-party arbitration. A mediated settlement is binding only if embodied in an agreement between the parties.

2.2.2.2 ODR or e-ADR v. traditional ADR

Whereas ADR moved dispute resolution 'out of court', ODR moves it even further away from court – to cyberspace.[23] Compared with traditional ADR, ODR or e-ADR has the following advantages:

- *Time and financial resources savings*: ODR allows parties who are located in multiple countries or different time zones, or who cannot agree on a joint meeting time, to converge at a single meeting point without travel and related expenses.
- *Flexibility*: ODR allows the parties to choose neutrals anywhere in the world. It no longer matters where expert neutrals reside, as ODR brings neutrals instantly in touch with the parties.

- *Speed*: ODR is faster in producing a resolution than traditional ADR, precisely because physical convergence is not necessary for meaningful interaction.[24]
- *Transparency and traceability*: Since ODR is significantly less expensive than other forms of dispute resolution, it opens the door to a wider range of disputes than do other dispute resolution institutions. But ODR is not merely a less expensive and more technologically advanced version of ADR; it differs from traditional ADR in substantial respects. Perhaps most importantly, it tends to be more transparent than some ADR processes. ODR, unlike ADR, is conducted through electronic communications and therefore leaves a digital trail. Since the information is transmitted online, it is preserved in digital form, and even after being 'deleted' can often be resurrected. The existence of ODR records heightens the element of traceability. In that sense, the records left by ODR are more permanent than those left by court trials, and are certainly better preserved than the oral face-to-face communications exchanged in traditional ADR. Furthermore, digital records may also serve as a check on the behaviour of mediators, parties and their representatives, even if no formal appeal procedure exists.[25]
- *Emotional control*: The lack of personal interaction in ODR can be an advantage in disputes in which the emotional involvement of the parties is so high that it is preferable that they do not see each other.[26]
- *Two additional parties*: There are two more parties involved than in traditional ADR, called the fourth party and the fifth party (see Figure 2.1).[27]

As shown in Figure 2.1, the two disputing parties are at the base of the pyramid. The third party is usually the facilitator, mediator or arbitrator. The fourth party is the technology, while the fifth party, at the top of the

Figure 2.1 ODR parties

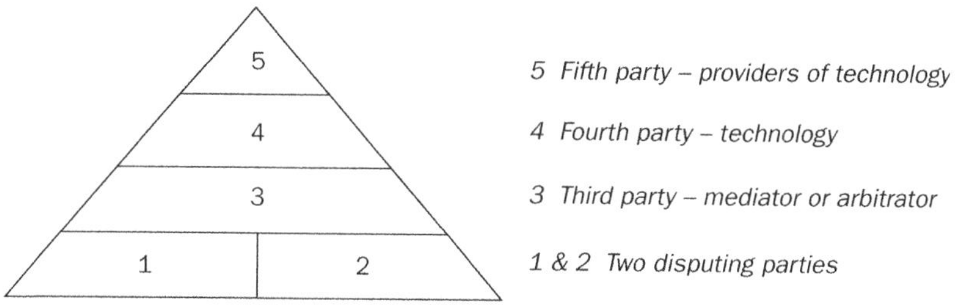

pyramid, is the provider of the technology. The fifth party, being the one who delivers the fourth party, is present in all ODRs. Sometimes, when third parties use general software, they become the provider of the technology. Mediators may also run general chat software on the website that they use to mediate between the parties. They then become a fifth party as well.

An important part of future analysis should concern the legal consequences of being a fifth party, and the legal duties this brings with it, such as information requirements the fifth party has to fulfil, liability of the fifth party in relation to the third party and/or the parties having a dispute, and possible contractual relationships between the fifth party and the other parties.[28]

2.2.2.3 Cybercourts v. traditional courts

Table 2.1 summarises the differences between online and offline court proceedings. Online court proceedings have a significant advantage over offline proceedings: convenience.[30] As with an e-ADR, the most obvious benefit of a cybercourt would be its technological capabilities. For example, the use of technology would bring efficiency to the court system. The management of court pleadings and other documents would be

Table 2.1 **Comparison of proceedings online (in cybercourts) and offline (in traditional courts)[29]**

	Online	Offline
Due process protections	No	Yes
Judicial supervision	No	Yes
Formal discovery	Independently, and only if lawsuit is field	Yes
Motions	No	Yes
Voir dire	Limited	Yes
Witness testimony	Summarised	Live
Binding outcomes	Limited	Yes
Nature of enforcement	By contract or agreement	By judgment
Number of jurors	By agreement or site rule	By court rule
Non-economic remedies	Yes	No
Right to appeal	No	Yes

streamlined. In addition, the use of technology would assist jurors, attorneys, their respective clients and witnesses. It would enable decision-makers to experience physical evidence in much the same manner as the disputing parties did at the time of the dispute, and lawyers to review information in a cybercase file at any convenient time. Likewise, witnesses could testify without actually going to a physical courtroom.[31]

The most compelling strength of online processes are as follows:

- They are useful in preparing parties to settle disputes in a fashion that is objectively defensible, consistent with what outsiders think the case is worth;[32] this is the most compelling strength.
- The cybercourt can be used in pre-trial preparation with no cost in preparing a case for a traditional trial.[33]
- Compared with negotiation and mediation, which may result in a settlement or nothing, cybercourt litigation can produce a judgment.
- Judicially mediated settlements are much easier to enforce because they qualify as 'consent judgments' or as another form of enforceable instrument.
- There is an element of publicity and accountability in courts that is lacking in private justice.[34]

These advantages tend to increase trust in the process. In an environment such as e-commerce, which lacks trust, cybercourts may thus play a useful role, supplemental to that of private ODR. They should thus be promoted not only for reasons of convenience, but because they foster confidence in e-commerce.[35] However, there are still downsides in an online proceeding, for example, lack of adequate access to high-technology internet tools; unbalanced users' technical skills; fraud and deception of evidence; and the quality of online decision-makers.[36] These are obstacles that legislators and practitioners must work on in the future. An example of online proceedings (www.i-courthouse.com) is given in Section 2.2.5.

2.2.2.4 E-negotiation v. e-mediation v. e-arbitration

Online negotiation, online mediation and online arbitration can also be called e-negotiation, e-mediation and e-arbitration, or cyber negotiation, cyber mediation and cyber arbitration. These terms are described in Figure 2.2.

As seen in Figure 2.2, arbitration is an adversarial procedure in which an independent third party decides the case, while mediation and

Figure 2.2 E-negotiation v. e-mediation v. e-arbitration

E-negotiation	*Automated negotiation* The parties successively submit to a computer a monetary figure as a settlement proposal. The computer then compares the offer and the demand and reaches a settlement for their arithmetic mean.
	Assisted negotiation The parties communicate with one another over the internet, using for instance e-mails, web-based communication tools or video conferences.
E-mediation	The online form of traditional mediation. A third neutral person with no decision power tries convincing the parties to reach an agreement (the only difference with offline mediation is that the third neutral person and the parties always communicate via the internet).
E-arbitration	Similar to traditional arbitration, in the sense that a third party chosen by the parties, or nominated by the institution chosen by the parties, renders a decision on the case after having heard the relevant arguments and seen the appropriate evidence.

negotiation are consensual procedures in which the disputants aim to reach agreement, either on their own or assisted by a third party called the mediator. However, they have something in common in that they all make use of online technology, exchanging and processing information as well as submitting documents via the internet. In short, it is a virtual procedure established in virtual cyberspace.

Although these three types of ODRs have their similarities, disputes should be resolved according to the most appropriate resolution. For instance, e-mediation is useful in cases:

- involving parties who desire a settlement but are reluctant or unable to meet one another directly;
- that involve highly confidential or proprietary information, such as disputes with trade secrets;
- in which the amount at stake is too low to litigate or arbitrate.[37]

2.2.3 ODR technology – three step-model

The ODR process, as a dispute resolution medium, is desired to be secure, efficient, flexible and user-friendly. It must be able to deal with the initial filing, neutral appointment, evidentiary processes, oral hearings, neutral executive sessions, and the rendering and transmittal of an award in binding processes.[38] It should be envisioned as a virtual space in which disputants have a variety of dispute resolution tools at their disposal. Participants can select any tool they consider appropriate for the resolution of their conflict and use the tools in any order or manner they desire, or they can be guided through the process.[39] The most effective ODR environment can be created by the three-step model:

> First, the negotiation support tool should provide feedback on the likely outcomes of the dispute if the negotiation were to fail – i.e. the 'best alternative to a negotiated agreement' (BATNA).
>
> Second, the tool should attempt to resolve any existing conflicts using dialogue techniques.
>
> Third, for those issues not resolved in step two, the tool should employ compensation/trade-off strategies in order to facilitate resolution of the dispute.
>
> Finally, if the result from step three is not acceptable to the parties, the tool should allow the parties to return to step two and repeat the process recursively until either the dispute is resolved or a statement occurs.[40]

At the early stage, to fulfil the ODR functions, Lodder developed an ODR software called 'DiaLaw', a two-player dialogue game designed to establish justified statements, which can clearly explain the basic logic of the ODR environment. A dialogue in DiaLaw starts when a player introduces a statement he or she wants to justify. The dialogue ends if the opponent accepts the statement (justified), or if the statement is withdrawn (not justified). A party using the argument tool can enter one of the following three types of statement:

> 1) Issue: A statement that initiates a discussion. At the moment of introduction, this statement is not connected to any other statement.
>
> 2) Supporting statement: Each statement entered by a party that supports statements of the same party.
>
> 3) Responding statement: Each statement entered by a party that responds to statements of the other party.[41]

2.2.3.1 Example of a DiaLaw formula

In response to the discussion above, here is an example of a DiaLaw formula and a simple scenario involving electronic contracting (see Figure 2.3).

Formula

The initial statement P(E, P(E)) sets out the issue of dispute, which is the only statement not connected to other statements when the dialogue game board opens, as it is the only statement not connected to other statements at the moment of opening the dialogue game board. The formula P(E, Q(C)) is used to summarise the actions of party P, who enters the statement E, in response to the connected claim C made previously by party Q.

Scenario

C: Claim

E: Statement by P – 'Our company wants to return your products'

P: Party P – Peter White Trading Company

Q: Party Q – Queen Computing Manufactory

P sued Q for breach of the electronic software sales contract.

Dialogue

Q ('We can't accept returned products', P ('Our company wants to return your products'))

P ('Your products lack "diary" function, which is in breach of our contract', Q ('We can't accept returned products'))

Q ('We can add the function to your products, or refund 2 per cent of the payment amount', P ('Your products lack "diary" function, which is in breach of our contract'))

Figure 2.3 ODR settlement

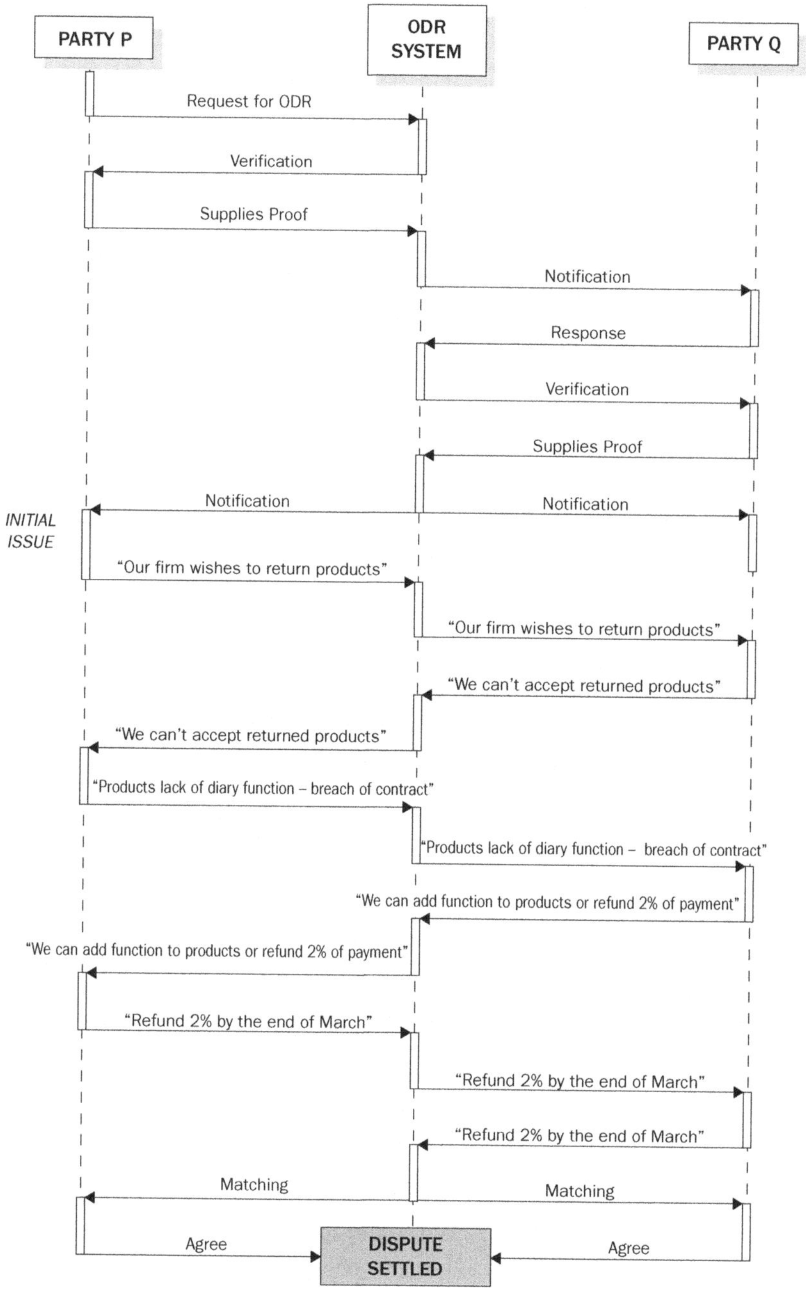
PARTY P
ODR SYSTEM
PARTY Q
Request for ODR
Verification
Supplies Proof
Notification
Response
Verification
Supplies Proof
Notification
Notification
INITIAL ISSUE
"Our firm wishes to return products"
"Our firm wishes to return products"
"We can't accept returned products"
"We can't accept returned products"
"Products lack of diary function – breach of contract"
"Products lack of diary function – breach of contract"
"We can add function to products or refund 2% of payment"
"We can add function to products or refund 2% of payment"
"Refund 2% by the end of March"
"Refund 2% by the end of March"
"Refund 2% by the end of March"
Matching
Matching
Agree
DISPUTE SETTLED
Agree

P ('Return 2 per cent of the payment by the end of March', Q ('We can add the function to your products, or refund 2 per cent of the payment amount'))

Q ('Return 2 per cent of the payment by the end of March', P ('Return 2 per cent of the payment by the end of March'))

Result

Q = P and P = Q → Dispute Settled

2.2.4 Hybrid process: med-arb two-step approach

Some ODR processes are a combination of separate ODR processes.[42] Mediation and arbitration (med-arb) is a mechanism of a hybrid process, in which disputed parties agree to use a blend of mediation and arbitration to handle their conflict. First, a mediator is in charge of the dispute mediating any disagreement between the parties. If the disputants refuse to accept the solutions, then the mediator acts as an arbitrator and decides the results of the remaining issues.[43]

The final result, therefore, combines both mediation settlement and adjudicatory processes. This two-step approach helps avoid throwing the conflict into the more cumbersome and time-consuming litigation process.[44] A successful example can be given by NovaForum,[45] which provides med-arb services through its Electronic Courthouse. Another successful example can be also provided by AAA-Cybersettle,[46] which combines online negotiation with the other online dispute resolutions. The mechanism of AAA-Cybersettle will be detailed in Section 4.2.3.

2.2.5 Online court proceedings: three-step process

Online court proceedings are similar to those offline. They allow peers to judge cases in ways identical to a live courtroom trial, incorporating most of the steps in the pre-trial and trial stages of litigation.[47] However, a difference from an offline courtroom is that the jury doesn't actually see the parties, nor do they interact with one another to any significant extent.[48] A sample online court proceeding is shown in Figure 2.4 (www.i-courthouse.com).

Figure 2.4 Online jury proceeding (www.i-courthouse.com)

```
                    File a case (case number: xxx)
                      │                    │
                      ▼                    ▼
            Plaintiff's trial book   Defendant's trial book
                      │                    │
             Opening statement      Opening statement
                      │                    │
             Plaintiff's exhibits   Defendant's exhibits
             (Testimony/Evidence)   (Testimony/Evidence)
                      │                    │
             Closing statement      Closing statement
                      │                    │
             Closing argument       Closing argument
                      │                    │
                      └────────┬───────────┘
                               ▼
            Jurors' questions, comments and verdicts
                               │
                               ▼
                        Trial results
```

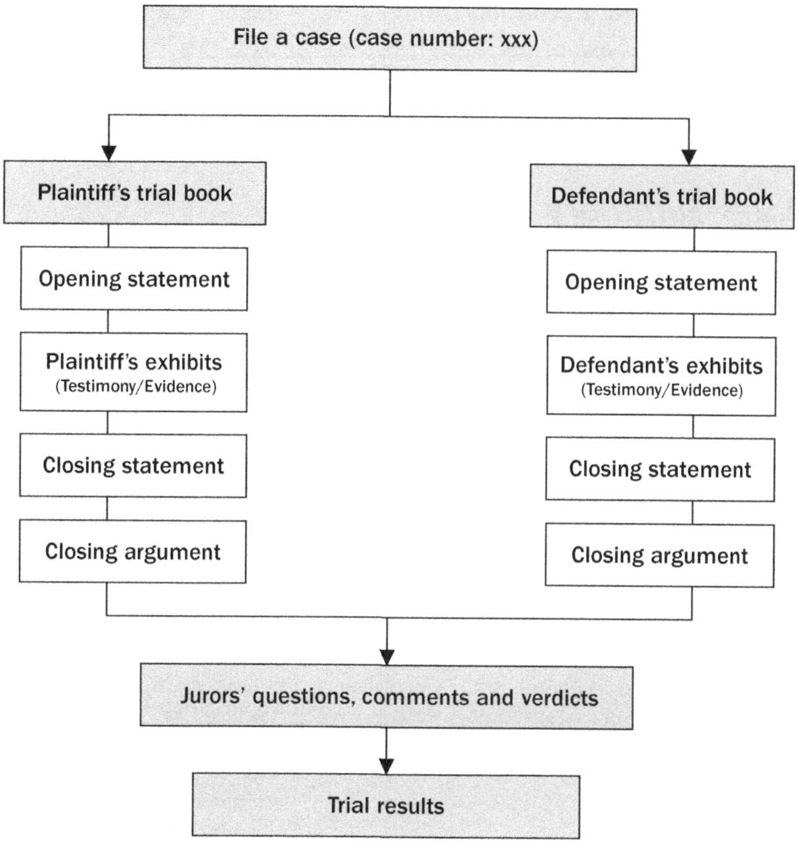

Case filing including statement, testimony, evidence and arguments can be submitted via interactive forms[49] located in the 'trial book'.[50] Evidence can take the form of any of the scanned documents, pictures, web pages, or e-mails sent and received. Finding a regular case at iCourthouse is free and so is being a juror. Lawyers can file a JurySmart case for under US$200 and receive thereafter a certified report with the trial outcomes.[51] Cases are open until closed by the plaintiff, when the parties agree there has been a final verdict or the parties have settled the case.[52] Alternatively, parties can leave a case for juror feedback indefinitely but may agree that only the verdicts given before a specific date and time will count or that only a specific number of the verdicts or verdicts entered during a particular period of will count.[53]

Anyone can register as a juror on iCourthouse, giving verdicts, comments and asking the disputants questions. In the author's view, at the early stage of a cybercourt, this opening might be a good idea to make everyone aware of and involved in the cybercourt system. However, as the e-court system gradually matures, in the next phase of its development guidelines should be drawn up for selecting jurors.

2.2.6 Summary of ODR methods

Table 2.2 shows a comparison of ODR methods.

Table 2.2 Comparison of ODR methods[54]

Main ODR methods	Negotiation	Mediation	Arbitration	Med-arb	Cybercourt
Type of process	Settlement	Settlement	Adjudicatory	Settlement and adjudicatory	Adjudicatory
Main online technologies	E-mail; software; bulletin boards and chat rooms	E-mail; list services; bulletin boards and chat rooms	E-mail; video conferencing; streaming video over web	E-mail; list services; bulletin boards; chat room; video conferencing and streaming video over web	Interactive forms and any methods used in med-arb
Role of third-party neutral	None	Mediator	Arbitrator	Mediator and arbitrator	Judge and juries
Nature of party participation	Voluntary	Voluntary or by agreement	Voluntary or by agreement	Voluntary or by agreement	By agreement only
Use of witnesses and documentary evidence	Not generally used	Not generally used	Allowed, but may be limited	Allowed, but may be limited	Generally used
Privacy of proceedings	Confidential	Confidential, unless otherwise agreed to by parties	Confidential, unless otherwise agreed to by parties	Confidential, unless otherwise agreed to by parties	Publicity (open hearing)

Table 2.2 Comparison of ODR methods[54] (*Cont'd*)

Main ODR methods	Negotiation	Mediation	Arbitration	Med-arb	Cybercourt
Nature of outcomes	Nonbinding, unless parties enter into settlement contract	Confidential, unless parties enter into settlement contract	May be nonbinding or binding with limited grounds for appeal, depending on party agreement	May be nonbinding or binding with limited grounds for appeal, depending on party agreement	Binding result or by party agreement
Enforcement of outcomes	By contract	By contract	Valid arbitration awards enforceable in court	By contract for mediation; valid arbitration awards enforcement in court	Judicial awards enforcement in court

Notes

1. Alvaro (2003), pp. 187, 188.
2. Ponte (2001), pp. 55, 60–1.
3. Zavaletta (2002), pp. 2, 5.
4. Tyler (2004), p. 6.
5. Katsh and Rifkin (2001), p. 5.
6. Ibid., p. 2.
7. ABA (2002b), p. 1.
8. NADRAC (2006), p. 105.
9. Edwards and Wilson (2007).
10. Exon (2002), pp. 1, 7.
11. Katsh and Rifkin (2001), p. 9.
12. Schultz (2004), pp. 71, 89.
13. Rule (2002), p. 174.
14. Symbolic capital is the recognition, institutionalised or not, that different agents receive from a group. A person, a body of persons, or an institution has symbolic capital if it is recognised by society as having characteristics that are valuable in a given field. See Schultz (2004), pp. 71, 90.
15. *Whelan* v. *Jaslow*, 609 F. Supp. 1307 (E.D. Pa, 1985); 797 F. 2d 1222 (3d Cir 1986); cert, denied 479 US 1031 (1987).
16. Katsh and Rifkin (2001), p. 25.
17. Ibid., p. 29.
18. Ibid.

19. Ponte and Cavenagh (2005), p. 12.
20. Ibid.
21. See http://www.squaretrade.com/cnt/jsp/prs/sd_tribune_111101.jsp (accessed 31 August 2007).
22. Ponte and Cavenagh (2005), p. 14.
23. Katsh and Rifkin (2001), p. 26.
24. Alvaro (2003), pp. 187, 189.
25. Rabinovich-Einy (2003–4), p. 1.
26. Lodder and Zeleznikow (2005), pp. 287, 302.
27. Lodder (2006), p. 143.
28. Ibid., pp. 143, 153.
29. Ponte and Cavenagh (2005), p. 103 (Chart 6.2 Comparison of Proceedings).
30. Kaufmann-Kohler and Schultz (2004), p. 40.
31. Exon (2002), pp. 1, 18–19.
32. Kaufmann-Kohler and Schultz (2004), p. 42.
33. Ibid.
34. Ibid.
35. Ibid.
36. Ponte and Cavenagh (2005), pp. 113–14.
37. Ibid., pp. 71–2.
38. Alvaro (2003), pp. 187, 188.
39. Lodder and Zeleznikow (2005), pp. 287, 300.
40. Ibid., p. 301.
41. Ibid., p. 305.
42. Ponte and Cavenagh (2005), p. 24.
43. Ibid.
44. Ibid.
45. See http://www.novaforum.com (accessed 28 September 2007).
46. See http://www.adr.org (accessed 28 September 2007).
47. Ponte and Cavenagh (2005), p. 102.
48. Ibid.
49. Ibid., pp. 102–7.
50. Trial books are those where you post the evidence and arguments for the claim; see for example http://www.i-courthouse.com (accessed 1 September 2008).
51. See http://www.i-courthouse.com.
52. Ponte and Cavenagh (2005), p. 104.
53. Ibid., pp. 104–5.
54. Ponte and Cavenagh (2005), p. 23 (Upgrade of 'Table 1–2: Summary of Main Characteristics of ODR Methods').

3

The current legal environment of ODR

3.1 International legislative developments

The internet brings together people who are operating under different legal systems and from widely disparate cultural backgrounds. Legislation is always a step behind practice, as the internet has grown and is still growing too fast for society to assimilate. Linguistic differences echo cultural differences and therefore translations often fail to bridge the gaps in parties' understandings and expectations. In conjunction with the above difficulties, there are also technical, social and political difficulties. How can international legislation take into account all these different legal systems and disparate cultural backgrounds?

Given the divergence of legal rules concerning jurisdiction and choice of law in different countries, it would be difficult at present to envisage creating an entity, such as a global online standards commission, that would have prescriptive, regulatory or enforcement jurisdiction. Jurisdictional complexity is thus a barrier to creating an international treaty-based entity to regular ODR providers.[1]

However, the existing UNCITRAL Model Law on International Commercial Arbitration[2] (see Appendix C) may, at this current stage, be useful to international online arbitration. Article 1 of the Model Law states that arbitration is international if:

> the parties to an arbitration agreement have, at the time of the conclusion of that agreement, their places of business in different states; or one of the following places is situated outside the State in which the parties have their places of business: (i) the place of arbitration if determined in, or pursuant to, the arbitration

agreement; (ii) any place where a substantial part of the obligations of the commercial relationship is to be performed or the place with which the subject-matter of the dispute is most closely connected; or (iii) the parties have expressly agreed that the subject-matter of the arbitration agreement relates to more than one country.

However, international online arbitration cannot truly come into its own as a recognised method of resolving disputes with the existing offline arbitration legislation, unless the international community can resolve nine major legal issues that online arbitration participants will face:

1. What form must an online arbitration agreement take?
2. Who should hear the dispute?
3. Where will arbitration occur?
4. What law will govern the online international arbitration?
5. Who will pay online arbitration costs and what will they consist of?
6. What time limits will govern online arbitration?
7. What evidentiary rules will govern online arbitration?
8. What form will the award take and how will it be enforced?
9. Is confidentiality feasible and advisable in online international arbitration?[3]

These are nine crucial issues, for which meaningful and uniform standards will have to be agreed by the global community to ensure the success of online international arbitration. The question of what law will apply in online disputes should be solved *prima facie* and according to simple and automatic rules. The UNCITRAL Arbitration Rules state that, unless agreed by the parties, the tribunal shall apply the law determined by 'the conflicts of laws rules, which it considers applicable'.[4] Another solution would be to impose on the parties in an online arbitration, or at least to suggest to them, that they give the arbitrator the powers of an 'amiable compositeur', thus apply an international *lex mercatoria*.[5]

The core issue out of the above nine questions is the uncertainty of 'e-awards', as it is very difficult to determine the place of arbitration or proceedings. In other words, is an electronic award rendered via the internet regarded as domestic or foreign?

This could in turn lead to a so-called 'floating arbitration', 'delocalisation of arbitration' or 'floating award'. Delocalised arbitration means that it is floating on the surface of legal systems of different countries, not attaching itself to any municipal legal order.[6] Delocalised arbitration is detached from the procedural rules and the substantive law of the place of arbitration; the procedural rules of any specific national law; and the national substantive law of any specific jurisdiction.[7] However, parties should incorporate a delocalised arbitration clause in their agreement so that the award could be eligible for enforcement.[8]

It is worth noticing that the New York Convention of 1958[9] covers delocalisation of arbitration as it does not limit its field of application to awards governed by national laws. Thus, an award generally can be enforced in a state that has ratified the convention. Furthermore, it is notable that Article 1(1)(a) of the New York Convention applies to awards not considered domestic or subject to the laws of another state. The fact that the award is rendered in some countries does not necessarily mean that it is a domestic award, as the nationality of an arbitral award might depend on the law governing the arbitral procedure. Therefore, the application of foreign rules or non-national substantive laws to the subject matter of the dispute could make an award international or foreign.

Currently, there are no uniform ODR rules with regard to online arbitral awards at the international level. In the author's view, there is need to detach online arbitration of such disputes from national law, both procedurally and substantively. It is suggested that the application of transnational substantive rules through denationalised online arbitration would be the pinnacle of autonomy of e-business and online arbitration.[10]

In the author's opinion, international ADR organisations need to work together to develop some basic standards for specialised ODR training and practice. Issues such as confidentiality, impartiality, conflicts of interest, ODR disclosure policies, educational and training requirements, linguistic and cultural skills, and adequate party representation need to be fully addressed and applied to ODR service providers.[11] In addition, there needs to be international cooperation and agreement on the enforcement, jurisdiction and choice of law issues of ODR settlements.

3.2 EU trends in ODR legislation

In the EU, Article 17 of the E-Commerce Directive is in favour of online dispute resolution, which requires that 'member states shall ensure that, in the event of disagreement between an information society service provider and the recipient of the service, their legislation does not hamper the use of out-of-court schemes, available under national law, for dispute settlement, including appropriate electronic means'.[12] In addition, it requires member states to 'encourage bodies, responsible for the out-of-court settlement of, in particular consumer disputes to operate in a way which provides adequate procedural guarantees for the parties concerned'[13] and to 'encourage bodies responsible for out-of-court dispute settlement to inform the Commission of the significant decision they take regarding Information Society services and to transmit any other information on the practices, usages, or customs relating to electronic commerce'.[14]

On 23 April 2008, the European Parliament formally approved, without amendments, the Council's common position on the new Mediation Directive – EC Directive of the European Parliament of Council on Certain Aspects of Mediation in Civil and Commercial Matters.[15] The new Directive – Directive 2008/52/EC of the European Parliament and of the Council of 21 May 2008 on certain aspects of mediation in civil and commercial matters (hereafter 'the Mediation Directive'; see Appendix B) – was published in the *Official Journal of the European Union* on 24 May 2008, entering into force on the twentieth day after it.[16] The purpose of the Directive is to facilitate access to dispute resolution, to encourage the use of mediation, and to ensure a sound relationship between mediation and judicial proceedings.[17]

The Mediation Directive is an achievement of regulating out-of-court dispute resolutions as it is in favour of electronic communications and, to an extent, ODR by encouraging the use of mediation in cross-border disputes and the use of modern communication technologies in the mediation process. This is reflected by recitals 8 and 9 of the Mediation Directive:

> (8) The provisions of this Directive should apply only to mediation in *cross-border* disputes, but nothing should prevent Member States from applying such provisions also to internal mediation processes.
>
> (9) This Directive should not in any way prevent the use of *modern communication technologies* in the mediation.[18]

Moreover, its favouring of ODR also reflects on the provisions of 'ensuring the quality of mediation'[19] and 'information for the general public'.[20]

For example, Article 4 of the Mediation Directive provides that 'Member States shall encourage, *by any means which they consider appropriate*, the development of, and adherence to, voluntary codes of conduct by mediators and organisations providing mediation services, as well as other effective quality control mechanism concerning the provision of mediation services'. Article 9 of the Mediation Directive explicitly indicates the use of the internet: 'Member States shall encourage, *by any means which they consider appropriate*, the availability to the general public, *in particular on the internet*, of information on how to contact mediators and organisations providing mediation services.'

There are two more merits of the Mediation Directive: to ensure the enforce ability of agreements resulting from mediation;[21] and to enhance the confidentiality of mediation.[22] The Directive enables parties to request a written agreement concluded following mediation. The content of the agreement is similar to a court judgment, which shall be made enforceable. For example, this can be achieved by way of 'a court or other competent authority in a judgment or decision or in an authentic instrument'.[23] The Directive ensures the confidentiality of mediation by preventing mediators or those involved in the mediation process from giving information or evidence in civil and commercial judicial proceedings or arbitration.[24] These two provisions are essential to boost parties' confidence in mediation.

With the development of the EU out-of-court dispute resolution legislative mechanisms, the EU online ADR practices have been progressing. An example of online ADR in the EU is provided by the Czech Arbitration Court, which is attached to the Economic Chamber of the Czech Republic and Agricultural Chamber of the Czech Republic. The Czech Arbitration Court was appointed by the European Registry of Internet Domain Names (EURid) on 12 April 2005 to provide ADR for .eu domain name disputes.[25] It sets up the ADR rules called '.eu Alternative Dispute Resolution Rules', which apply to all complaints filed on or after 7 December 2005.[26] The Czech Arbitration Court is now able to administer .eu ADR proceedings in practically all official EU languages. The online platform of the Czech Arbitration Court has been translated in these languages, and a complaint can be filed in almost any official EU language; translation of the remaining languages is well under way. The online ADR platform can be illustrated as the following steps:

- Register yourself as a new user by clicking on the button 'Register New User'.
- Log in to the online platform.

- Start a new dispute by clicking on the button 'Start New Dispute'.
- Choose the language and then click 'File the Form'.
- Fill out the complaint form.
- Send the complaint automatically to the Czech arbitration by clicking 'File Complaint'.

At any time during the ADR proceeding it is possible to change your personal details by clicking on 'My Menu' and then 'Change of user details'. It is possible as well to add a representative or change the information given to that person by following the links 'My Menu' and then 'My Representatives', and selecting the options to add or edit.[27]

Although ADR.eu is just applicable to domain names, these ADR rules and the online ADR service platform sets a good example for the new online ADR service in the future. The most successful ADR service is provided by the World Intellectual Property Organisation (WIPO), which is the first domain name dispute resolution service provider to be accredited by ICANN, and the first to receive a case under the Uniform Domain Name Dispute Resolution Policy (UDRP).[28] The WIPO provider is successful because it is time and cost effective, and can enforce the outcomes of domain names disputes. The outcome of domain name cases is limited to the transfer or cancellation of the domain name. Cases can be decided by panellists appointed by the Centre or by the parties from a special WIPO list. Transfer decisions are implemented directly by domain name registrars.[29] In the author's opinion, ODR providers can register a website such as 'odr.eu' or 'edispute.eu', providing dispute resolutions to wider e-commerce disputes, for instance, electronic contracts. Moreover, the WIPO ADR centre, and eu.ADR rules and its web service can become a vital model for proposing an overarching ODR regulation in the EU.

3.3 US ODR regulations

In the US providers of ODR are increasingly facing calls for self-regulation and adoption of best practice guidelines. During summer 2002 the ABA Task Force on Electronic Commerce and Alternative Dispute Resolution addressed the final recommendations and report on disputes in e-commerce.[30] The report emphasises that an ODR transaction is indeed an e-commerce transaction in and of itself. Thus, as internet merchants, ODR providers should adhere to adequate standards and codes of conduct. The ABA essentially recommends that ODR providers strive to achieve transparency through information and disclosure as a basis to achieve sustainability. These recommended best practices contain many principles that apply in both B2B and B2C disputes. It is recommended to enable disputants to make intelligent choices concerning ODR providers, to help give them confidence in the efficacy of ODR and therefore to encourage the disputants to use ODR as a means of obtaining resolution of their complaints.[31] The recommended course of action includes:[32]

- publishing statistical reports;
- employing identifiable and accessible data formats;
- presenting printable and downloadable information;
- publishing decisions with whatever safeguards to prevent party identification;
- describing the types of services provided;
- affirming due process guarantees;
- disclosing minimum technology requirements to use the provider's technology;
- disclosing all fees and expenses to use ODR services;
- disclosing qualifications and responsibilities of neutrals;
- disclosing jurisdiction, choice of law and enforcement clauses, for example, ODR providers should disclose the jurisdiction where complaints against the ODR provider can be brought, and any relevant jurisdictional limitations.

The Task Force believes that the types of disclosures outlined in the recommendations will help to instil confidence and trust in the new ODR industry and marketplace.[33]

The iADR Centre, a non-profit, educational and informational entity, is also recommended by the Task Force. The iADR Centre is most likely to gain traction with various stakeholders including government entities, internet merchants, ODR service providers and consumers at this juncture. At present, the Task Force has recommended the creation of a web-based entity that would perform the following tasks:

1) Disseminate information concerning the Recommended Best Practices, along with information concerning existing ODR codes of practice;

2) List and provide information concerning the available ODR/ADR service providers available for the resolution of e-commerce disputes;

3) Develop and/or disseminate sample complaints handling, privacy and best practices forms, codes, standards, and guidelines; and;

4) Provide all information on a multilingual basis via the World Wide Web.[34]

In addition, to perform the above tasks efficiently, the Task Force also suggests that this entity should be consistent with official statements of the US and EU governments. In the author's view, the successful establishment of the iADR Centre will be a leading worldwide ODR private organisation, which performs a similar function to the ICC in the future, and will help to boost users' e-confidence and trust.

The Centre for Information Technology and Dispute Resolution of University of Massachusetts Amherst offers a complete and updated list of ODR providers around the world.[35] Four examples are given below.

Blind bidding

Blind bidding systems allow parties in a dispute to submit settlement offers to a computer, and if the offers are within a certain range, often 30 per cent of each other, the parties agree to settle and split the difference.[36] Cybersettle and clickNsettle provide successful blind bidding services. For example, the clickNsettle website[37] allows many rounds of offers and counteroffers within a specified period of time. To ensure that the negotiations take place in good faith, parties are required to increase (or decrease) their offer (or counteroffer) by a specified percentage over their previous offer (or counteroffer). If a settlement is not reached within the specified time period, then the offers expire and the cyber-negotiation fails.[38]

What is attractive about blind bidding is that if no settlement is reached, the offers are never revealed to the other party. This is intended to encourage parties to be more truthful about what their 'bottom line' might be.[39] The parties are, of course, free to resubmit their claim or move forward with another dispute resolution mechanism, such as mediation, arbitration or even litigation.

Cyber negotiation

SmartSettle,[40] originally called OneAccord, is a much more sophisticated negotiation software than the blind bidding systems. SmartSettle is intended for use in disputes that are simple or complex, single issue or multi-issue, two party or multi-party, composed of quantitative or qualitative issues, of short or long duration, and involving interdependent factors and issues.[41]

Cyber mediation

SquareTrade[42] and Internet Neutral website[43] are examples of cyber mediation. Internet Neutral allows parties to choose from several online mediation alternatives, including e-mail, instant messaging, chat conference rooms and video conferencing. Internet Neutral uses conferencing software that enables the mediator to communicate with the parties in designated channels or 'rooms' accessed securely with passwords. During the mediation, the software enables the parties to communicate through two channels: one for a private dialogue between one party and the mediator, the other for open dialogue with all participants, including the mediator.[44]

Cyber arbitration

AAA Webfile[45] is organised by the American Arbitration Association (AAA), providing internet-based arbitration services. Using the AAA Webfile, the disputants are required:

- to register as a new user;
- to enter claimant or claimant representative information as well as the respondent or respondent representative information;
- to enter the claim information and the claim summary;
- to submit their credit card payment.

The third step is a core procedure. The claim information includes the selection of the set of rules to apply and whether the disputant is filing an arbitration or mediation. Once they choose online arbitration, disputants need to select the numbers of arbitrators required for their claim, to review their arbitration clause to see if the number of arbitrators is addressed, and then to enter the contract date and the city and state of the hearing locale they prefer.

Compared with cyber negotiation and mediation, cyber arbitration is more complicated, strict and expensive, so there are fewer online arbitration service providers. But whatever methods the disputants choose, the most significant concern is whether ODR providers they are with are offering quality conflict resolution services. If ODR providers apply to the formal standards for the practice of ODR, such as the best practice guidelines, and take part in the uniform specialised training for ODR practitioners, for example, with the iADR Centre, it will provide the disputants with a level of confidence about their ODR provider regarding basic standards of quality and fairness.

3.4 Asian ODR legal practices

3.4.1 Singapore

Singapore, as the island was developed by the British East India Company, became a key trading port and multi-cultural country with immigrants from China, India and neighbouring regions. The establishment of Singapore laws requires 'due attention to the several religions, manners and usages of the native inhabitants'.[46] The Singapore legal system has its roots in the English legal system. Although modifications have been implemented in recent years, substantive English law still has strong influence on the Singapore legal system.[47]

In the field of ADR, Singapore has made considerable progress in modern society. There are three main out of court dispute resolution centres in Singapore: the Small Claims Tribunals (SCT), Singapore International Arbitration Centre (SIAC) and Singapore Mediation Centre (SMC).

3.4.1.1 Tribunals

The Small Claims Tribunals, subordinate courts of Singapore, were established in 1985 to provide a quick and inexpensive dispute resolution forum. The Tribunals have jurisdiction to hear claims that do not exceed SGD 10,000 in general, relating to contract disputes of the sale of goods, the provision of services, or tortuous damage to property.[48] In 1995 the jurisdiction of the Tribunals was extended to SGD 5,000, and in 1997 it was extended to SGD 20,000 where both parties to the dispute consent in writing.[49] In the subordinate courts, a form of court-based mediation known as Court Dispute Resolution was introduced in 1994. CDR is a voluntary settlement process in favour of a win–win situation, which allows parties to decide for themselves the terms of the settlement with the aid of a neutral third person, the Settlement Judge.[50]

3.4.1.2 Arbitration

The UNCITRAL Model Law on International Commercial Arbitration is the cornerstone of Singapore's law on international commercial arbitration. Singapore is also a party to the New York Convention 1958 on enforcement of arbitration awards. Founded in 1991, the Singapore International Arbitration Centre (SIAC)[51] offers a neutral and independent dispute resolution service for domestic and international cases. It comprises over 190 legal and industry experts in a broad range of subject areas.[52] It is noticeable that the SIAC supports electronic communications or online arbitration, as it can be evidenced on Rule 18.2 of Arbitration Rules of the Singapore International Arbitration Centre (hereafter 'the SIAC Rule 2007') – 'the Tribunal may hold hearings and meetings *by any means it considers expedient or appropriate* and at any location it considers convenient or appropriate'.[53] In addition, Article 4(3)(b) of the Singapore Arbitration Act 2001 also recognises electronic means of communication by providing that an arbitration agreement shall be in writing being contained in 'an exchange of letters, telex, telefacsimile or *other means of communication* which provide a record of the agreement'.[54]

3.4.1.3 Mediation

Mediation as a form of conflict resolution and dispute settlement is an inherent practice in many cultures. For that reason, mediation can be said to have been practised in Singapore ever since it had its first human habitants. Singapore's official ADR movement began in 1994 when judicial and academic institutions began programmes to promote mediation as a form of dispute settlement.[55] The Singapore Mediation Centre (SMC) was launched in 1997 to provide dispute settlements, including mediation, neutral evaluation, mediation-arbitration ('med-arb') and the Singapore Domain Name Dispute Resolution. It also provides training and accreditation for mediators as well as consultancy services for dispute prevention, management and resolution.[56]

3.4.1.4 Online ADR

Developed by the Singapore Academy of Law (SAL) and the SMC, DisputeManager.com was launched on 31 July 2002, funded by the Singapore government. It is an internet portal that allows for the settlement of disputes through online mediation, neutral evaluation and e-settlement.[57] It also provides dispute resolution service for '.sg' registrants.[58] Another online dispute resolution centre 'e@dr' is an initiative by the subordinate courts to help parties resolve disputes, especially those arising from e-commerce transactions.[59] It was established in 2000. Using e@dr, both the complainant and the person against whom a complaint is filed must have e-mail addresses. Then, the complainant has to complete a request for mediation form, which is sent by the moderator or administrator of e@dr to the responding party. The responding party completes a response form if he or she agrees to resolve the dispute by e@dr. Finally, the moderator suggests an appropriate dispute resolution method and mediator.[60]

As discussed above, most of the eADR services in Singapore are authorised or funded by Singapore governmental organisations. This type of ODR centre helps to boost disputers' confidence in using online dispute settlement mechanisms, especially at the early stage of the ODR development. However, when ODR services get more and more mature, the Singapore government should encourage private ODR providers to be established. The opening of ODR markets will benefit providers and users, as disputers can make a comparison between different ODR providers and choose the one that benefits them the most, which will urge ODR providers to improve their services.

3.4.2 China

3.4.2.1 Arbitration

In China, on 31 August 1994 the Chinese National People's Congress promulgated the Arbitration Law, with the aim of establishing a coherent nationwide arbitral system; it entered into force on 1 September 1995. In accordance with the Arbitration Law, establishment of online arbitrations is subject to the restrictions and requirements for market entry. For example, arbitration commissions are registered with the local judicial administrative department and organised by the local government and the chamber of commerce.[61] An arbitration commission has its own name, domicile and charter; possesses the necessary property; and has its own staff and arbitrators for appointment.[62] An arbitration commission comprises a chairman, two or four vice-chairmen and seven to eleven members. The arbitration commission appoints fair and honest persons as its arbitrators.[63]

Arbitration commissions are members of the China Arbitration Association, which is a self-regulatory organisation of arbitration commissions responsible for maintaining professional discipline among the commissions. They supervise the arbitration commissions, their members and arbitrators in accordance with the charter. Thus, if an ODR service provider really intends to label its service as 'arbitration', it would have to select carefully the location of its headquarters, obtain approval from local government and the chamber of commerce, apply to the competent authority for registration provided that it has fulfilled all the conditions of formation, and become a member of the China Arbitration Association.[64]

In the author's opinion, since ODR is borderless, the arbitration commission registration methods in China are too restrictive. The Arbitration Law in 1995 is not practical in the new age of cyber arbitration. There should be uniform online arbitration or even ODR registration regulation in national legislation to avoid the differences of local governments' policies.

3.4.2.2 Mediation

Mediation is popular in China, which is evidenced by culture and legislation. For centuries, mediation or conciliation has been widely used in China as an effective means to resolve disputes in the community.[65] The culture of mediation in China is different from the West. Traditionally, the Chinese concept of mediation has deep roots in Confucian philosophy, ideals such as harmony, peace and stability. In ancient China, people who had high prestige would put the disputing parties together and talk them into an agreement. This is the way of promoting a peaceful environment and advocating a harmonious society without conflicts. It may be characterised as a flexible and blended procedure of concessions, arrangements and compromises, though at other times it may take on some of the compelling aspects of adjudication.[66]

In modern China, the non-confrontational feature of mediation still demonstrates its unique advantage in commercial dispute resolution, especially in the handling of disputes in any ongoing relationships.[67] The China International Economic and Trade Arbitration Commission (CIETAC) and the China Maritime Arbitration Commission (CMAC) concluded 410 foreign-related commercial arbitration cases in 2000 and 27.32 per cent of these cases were settled by means of conciliation.[68]

Therefore, almost one-third of the commercial disputes were settled by conciliation or mediation rather than arbitration.

Chinese legislation also supports mediation in civil and commercial disputes. For example, Article 51 of the Civil Procedure Law of the People's Republic of China[69] permits the parties to 'reach a compromise of their own consent'. Article 49 of the Arbitration Law of the People's Republic of China[70] stipulates that parties may reach a private settlement even after the commencement of arbitration proceedings. Moreover, Article 8 of the Sino–America Agreement on Trade Relations states that:

> The Contracting Parties encourage the prompt and equitable settlement of any disputes arising from or in relation to contracts between their respective firms, companies and corporations, and trading organisations, through friendly consultations, conciliation or other mutually acceptable means.

Article 25 of the Law of the People's Republic of China on Chinese-foreign Contractual Joint Ventures[71] also provides that:

> Any dispute between the Chinese and foreign parties arising from the execution of the contract or the articles of the association for a contractual joint venture shall be settled through consultation or mediation.

On 5 May 1989 the state Council enacted the Organic Regulations on the People's Mediation Committee, which entered into force on the same date. An online mediation process may be established without any legal barriers from the Organic Regulations on the People's Mediation Committee, after obtaining all the necessary approval to establish an enterprise and registering with competent authorities. This seems to comply with the electronic free market entry principle. However, it is doubtful whether Chinese legislation has taken sufficient measures to ensure confidentiality and privacy in online mediation.[72] In the author's view, this should be a significant point of focus for any future ODR regulations.

3.4.2.3 Online ADR

In the digital era the Chinese cultural background will most certainly influence people's behaviour when using online dispute resolution. It has given some thought to legislators that ODR providers should be obliged to express and teach the terms and conditions of mediation before participants use it, because the ODR users can understand the functions of mediation and better use the system, and it will reduce the possibility of further confusion and miscommunication.

China Electronic Commerce Legal Network Company in conjunction with China Legal and Political Committee of Electronic Commerce established the first general China Online Dispute Resolution Centre (China ODR) and its website in 2000. This ODR Centre specialises in two services: online negotiation and online mediation. Any of the disputants can register their case online and apply for online dispute resolution. The Centre will then notify the other party through electronic means. If the other party agrees to use the online dispute mechanism, both parties will have to choose one of the dispute resolution methods, online negotiation or online mediation, and then start their procedures.[73]

China has gained experience in resolving '.cn' (ccTLD) domain name disputes via an ODR platform since 1997. On 30 September 2002 the China Internet Network Information Center (CNNIC) approved and implemented the CNNIC Domain Name Dispute Resolution Policy (CNDRP). The new amended CNDRP came into force on 17 March 2006. The CNDRP also set up an ODR system in China. Its service providers – the China International Economic and Trade Arbitration Commission (CIETAC) and Hong Kong International Arbitration Centre (HKIAC) – have established the online case management systems. However, if disputed domain names are gTLDs (for example .com and .org), they will be filed with the Asian Domain Name Dispute Resolution Centre (ADNDRC) instead of the Hong Kong International Arbitration Centre (HKIAC).[74] With these two ODR service providers, the complainant should submit the complaint form and submit it by e-mail.[75] Generally, a decision should be made on the basis of the statements and documents submitted by the parties. A panel has 14 days to render a decision.[76] The panel's decision will be submitted both in electronic and paper form signed by all the panellists. The decisions will be published on the websites of the service providers except for special circumstances.[77] In the author's opinion, the CIETAC and HKIAC ODR services are valuable experiments and cornerstones for developing Chinese ODR system for disputes arising from e-commerce transactions.

3.5 The Australian ODR legislative framework

Since Europeans arrived, Australian history has been enthused with notions of individualism. The ADR innovations have thus been influenced by a range of processes, incorporated with the history of collective dispute management, especially in the industrial relations system. A study reveals that non-litigious forms of dispute management have been practised in Australia since colonial times through arbitration provisions inherited from English law and the establishment of informal tribunal and ombudsmen systems. In the late 1960s and 1970s the focus was on tribunal systems and arbitration. Mediation-based approaches did not begin until the late 1970s.[78] In 1986 Australian Commercial Disputes Centre Limited (ACDC) was established to manage major commercial disputes and to divert them from courts. It was established as an independent, not-for-profit organisation assisted by the government, promoting and advancing excellence in ADR practice, innovation and education to the legal and business communities.[79]

In 1995 the National Alternative Dispute Resolution Advisory Council (NADRAC), a non-statutory body appointed by the Attorney-General, was established to 'advise the Government and federal courts and tribunals on ADR issues with a view to achieving and maintaining a high quality, accessible, integrated federal ADR system'.[80] It is funded by the Australian Government Attorney-General's Department. Recently the NADRAC released a report called 'Legislating for Alternative Dispute Resolution' to the Attorney-General of Australia.[81] It identifies the key issues policy-makers need to consider when incorporating ADR processes into new or existing legislation and assists in achieving appropriate standards and consistency in the legislative framework for ADR.[82] There is a debate on whether there is a need for legislation of ADR. In other words, should ADR be regulated under codes of practice and self-regulation mechanisms or under the principal act and regulations?

Currently, Australian law on arbitration is based on international conventions, legislation and common law or judge made law.[83] At the federal level, Australia has the International Arbitration Act 1974 (IAA), while the states and territories of Australia all have their own uniform legislation on arbitration – the Commercial Arbitration Act (CAA). The IAA gives effect to the Convention on the Recognition and Enforcement of Foreign Arbitral Awards 1958 (the New York Convention)[84] and the UNCITRAL Model Law on International Commercial Arbitration of 1985 (Appendix C).[85] However, section 21 of the IAA provides that the parties may exclude the application of the Model Law. Thus where the arbitration is not international or where the parties have excluded the application of the Model Law the CAA will apply.[86] The states and territories of Australia all have their codes of practice for mediation.

The NADRAC has been promoting online ADR since 2001. It has discussed and advised ADR in e-commerce. In 2001 the online ADR background paper from the NADRAC suggested that policy-makers should think globally but act locally to meet the challenges of online ADR, therefore, the NADRAC needs to make contact with similar bodies overseas, to seek information from local ODR practitioners and agencies in order to examine technology and risk using ODR mechanisms, and to review its recommendations and positions on ADR definitions, criteria, diversity and standards.[87] In 2006 the NADRAC formed definitions of ODR and ADR in a glossary of ADR terms in its guide to government policy-makers and legal drafters.[88]

There are not many successful private ODR services in Australia; however, the eCourt founded by the Federal Court of Australia in 2001 is a remarkable achievement of facilitating electronic communications in resolving disputes. The Federal Court of Australia is the first court in Australia to introduce such an initiative, establishing functional systems such as Casetrack, eSearch, eFiling, eCourtroom, eCase Administration, Electronic Trials, Electronic Appeals, Electronic Courtrooms and Hearings, Document Management System and Video Conferencing etc.[89]

There are two major successes of the eCourt systems: the introduction of electronic courtroom (eCourtroom) and the establishment of electronic filing system (eFiling). The eCourtroom is very simple and easy to use as it is an e-mail service within a secure environment. Using eCourtroom, case documents or evidence attached and sent out on the system can only be viewed by participants. The eFiling system incorporated with the eCourtroom makes sure that all documents sent electronically are capable of being printed with the content and in the form in which they were created using the Court's home page. Under the electronic filing system, authority applications and other documents are filed or lodged electronically with the Court. It is suggested that where a document must be signed, a facsimile of the signature may be affixed on the document by electronic means, or a document with the signature should be scanned and converted to an image format such as TIF, GIF or JPG.[90] In the author's view, the Australian eCourt is a success in resolving disputes online. It provides a model system for the development of private ODR services in the future in Australia.

Notes

1. ABA with Shidler Center for Law (2002).
2. UNCITRAL Model Law on International Commercial Arbitration 2006.
3. Witt (2001), pp. 441, 442.
4. UNCITRAL Model Law on International Commercial Arbitration 2006, Article 28.
5. Witt (2001), pp. 441, 452.
6. Janićijević (2005), p. 63.
7. Ibid., pp. 63, 64.
8. *Beaufort Developments (NI) Ltd* v. *Gilbert-Ash N.I. Ltd*, (1998) 2 WLR 860 (Eng.).
9. Convention on the Recognition and Enforcement of Foreign Arbitral Awards – the 'New York' Convention, 1958, available at http://www.uncitral.org/pdf/english/texts/arbitration/NY-conv/XXII_1_e.pdf (accessed 19 May 2008).
10. Patrikios (2006–7), pp. 271, 282.
11. Ponte (2001), pp. 55, 87.
12. Directive 2000/31/EC (Directive on Electronic Commerce), Article 17(1).
13. Ibid., Article 17(2).
14. Ibid., Article 17(3).
15. Council of the European Union, Directive 2008/.../EC.
16. Directive 2008/52/EC (the Mediation Directive).
17. EC (2008).
18. Directive 2008/52/EC (the Mediation Directive), recitals 8 and 9.
19. Ibid., Article 4.
20. Ibid., Article 9.
21. Ibid., Recital 19 and Article 6.
22. Ibid., Recital 23 and Article 7.
23. Ibid., Article 6(2).
24. Ibid., Article 7(1).
25. See http://www.adreu.eurid.eu/about_us/court/index.php (accessed 11 April 2006).
26. 'EU Alternative Dispute Resolution Rules' (the 'ADR Rules'), available at http://www.adr.eu (accessed 11 April 2006).
27. See http://www.adreu.eurid.eu/index.php (accessed 11 April 2006).
28. WIPO (n.d.), 'Guide to WIPO Domain Name Dispute Resolution'.
29. WIPO (n.d.), 'Dispute Resolution for the 21st Century'.
30. ABA with Shidler Center for Law (2002).
31. Ibid., pp. 415, 444.
32. Ibid., pp. 415, 458.
33. Ibid., pp. 415, 445.
34. Ibid., pp. 415, 450.
35. See http://www.ombuds.org/center/index.html.
36. Katsh and Rifkin (2001), p. 61.
37. See http://www.clicknsettle.com (accessed 30 March 2006).
38. Ponte (2002), pp. 441, 442–4.
39. Katsh and Rifkin (2001), p. 61.

40. See http://www.smartsettle.com (accessed 8 May 2007).
41. Katsh and Rifkin (2001), p. 62.
42. See http://www.squaretrade.com (accessed 9 May 2007).
43. See http://www.internetneutral.com (accessed 30 March 2006).
44. Goodman (2003), p. 4.
45. See http://www.odr.org (accessed 6 April 2006).
46. Woon (1988), p. 114.
47. Pryles (2006), p. 355.
48. ADR Advisory Committee Secretariat, available at http://notesapp.internet.gov.sg/__48256FAF0034EC9C.nsf/ (accessed 24 May 2008).
49. Claims of SGD 5,000–10,000 may be heard by the Small Claims Tribunal provided that the parties have agreed to this in a signed memorandum (Small Claims Tribunal Act, Section 5).
50. See http://app.subcourts.gov.sg/subcourts/page.aspx?pageid=4419 (accessed 22 Aug 2008).
51. See http://www.siac.org.sg/ (accessed 24 May 2008).
52. ADR Advisory Committee Secretariat, available at http://notesapp.internet.gov.sg/__48256FAF0034EC9C.nsf/ (accessed 24 May 2008).
53. Arbitration Rules of the Singapore International Arbitration Centre, 3rd ed., 1 July 2007, available at http://www.siac.org.sg/ (accessed 24 May 2008).
54. The Singapore Arbitration Act 2001, available at http://www.jus.uio.no/lm/singapore.arbitration.act.2001/toc.html (accessed 24 May 2008).
55. Pryles (2006), p. 387.
56. ADR Advisory Committee Secretariat, available at http://notesapp.internet.gov.sg/__48256FAF0034EC9C.nsf/ (accessed 24 May 2008).
57. Singapore Mediation Centre; see http://www.mediation.com.sg/disputemanager.htm (accessed 25 May 2008).
58. Singapore Network Information Centre; see http://www.nic.net.sg/sub_domain_disputes/faq.html (accessed 25 May 2008).
59. The Subordinate Courts of Singapore; see http://app.subcourts.gov.sg/e-adr/index.aspx (accessed 25 May 2008).
60. See http://app.subcourts.gov.sg/e-adr/page.aspx?pageid=3891 (accessed 25 May 2008).
61. Article 10 of the Arbitration Law of the People's Republic of China, adopted at the 8th Session of the Standing Committee of the 8th National People's Congress and promulgated on 31 August 1994, available at http://english.sohu.com/2004/07/04/78/article220847885.shtml (accessed 4 September 2007).
62. Arbitration Law of the People's Republic of China, Article 11.
63. Ibid., Article 13.
64. Xue (2004), pp. 377, 380.
65. Tao (2005), p. 1012.
66. Xue (2004), pp. 377, 390.
67. Tao (2005), pp. 1012–13.
68. Ibid., p. 1401.
69. Adopted at the Fourth Session of the Seventh National People's Congress on 9 April 1991; promulgated and effective by Order No. 44 of the President of the People's Republic of China as of 9 April 1991.

70. Adopted at the Eighth Session of the Standing Committee of the Eighth National People's Congress; promulgated on 31 August 1994 and effective as of 1 September 1995.
71. Adopted by the First Session of the Standing Committee of the Seventh National People's Congress on 13 April 1988; promulgated and revised by the Eighteenth Session of the Standing Committee on the Ninth National People's Congress on 31 October 2000.
72. Xue (2003), p. 16.
73. See http://www.odr.com.cn/ (accessed 3 September 2007).
74. Wang (2007), p. 7.
75. See http://dn.hkiac.org/cn/cne_complaint_form.html (accessed 24 May 2008).
76. Article 37 of the Rules for CNNIC Domain Name Dispute Resolution Policy, available at http://dn.hkiac.org/cn/cne_rules_procedure.html (accessed 25 May 2008).
77. Article 44 of the Rules for CNNIC Domain Name Dispute Resolution Policy, available at http://dn.hkiac.org/cn/cne_rules_procedure.html (accessed 25 May 2008).
78. Spencer and Brogan (2006), p. 30.
79. See http://www.acdcltd.com.au/ (accessed 26 May 2008).
80. See http://www.nadrac.gov.au/agd/WWW/disputeresolutionhome.nsf/Page/About_NADRAC (accessed 26 May 2008).
81. NADRAC (2006).
82. Ibid., pp. 1, 3.
83. Pryles (2006), p. 66.
84. Australia Federal International Arbitration Act 1974, Part II.
85. Ibid., Part III.
86. Pryles (2006).
87. NADRAC (2001).
88. NADRAC (2006), p. 99.
89. Federal Court of Australia, 'The eCourt Strategy', available at http://www.fedcourt.gov.au/ecourt/ecourt_strategy.html#overview (accessed 27 May 2008).
90. Federal Court of Australia, 'The Electronic Filing System', available at http://www.fedcourt.gov.au/ecourt/ecourt_efs_information.html (accessed 27 May 2008).

Analysis: learning from successful experiences

ODR, defined as both cybercourts and an extension of ADR, is important not only because it is successful in using speedy and cost-effective techniques to resolve cross-border disputes, but because it creates trust and confidence in making electronic commercial transactions in the e-marketplace, as it reduces the risk that e-commerce users are left with no redress if contracts are not performed.

A continuing challenge and demand for resolving cross-border commercial disputes resulting from globalisation calls for improving and modernising ODR services both in public and private sectors. How to guide newly launched ODR service providers to the successful practice will be a focal point in the development of ODR communities. Therefore pioneering experiences must be examined and understood.

4.1 Cybercourts

> Computer and Internet technology present challenges for the courts, as well as many potential benefits: Internet access to court information, electronic filing, payment of court obligations.[1]

Cybercourts provide dispute resolution services, both litigation and court-based ADR, using electronic communications. They generate confidence among the general public and their users because:

- They have tangible features: such a court is held in a building, thereby providing many points of reference and history indicating that it can be trusted.
- Judges already have a well-established reputation and the courts are very well integrated in many social contexts.

- Courts are a reference in society because they are integrated into an already existing architecture of confidence.[2]

An example of a successful cybercourt is the Michigan cybercourt, created by the Michigan Supreme Court under Public Act 262 of 2001 and operating since October 2002. It aims to develop technology throughout Michigan's judiciary and to be a forum for 'swift resolution of business and commercial actions, including those involving information technology, software, or web site development, maintenance or hosting'.[3]

The court is mobile and virtual, with no fixed locations, and it uses various legal technologies to store, share and present evidence over the internet between lawyers, ADR providers and courts. It recommends a series of e-court mechanisms, such as e-filing, a document management system, a case management system, an evidence and media presentation system, teleconferencing, video conferencing and digital recording.[4] The Michigan cybercourt collaborates with high-tech companies and employs highly educated staff. Instead of holding hearings in person, arguments and testimony can be presented via teleconference; evidence can be evaluated through streaming video or digital still images.[5]

According to the 2001 Michigan Public Act 262, the cybercourt has concurrent jurisdiction over commercial litigation in disputes where the amount in controversy exceeds US$25,000.[6] Judges appointed to sit on the cybercourt should have either commercial litigation experience or an interest in technology.[7] Parties who participate in the cybercourt are deemed to have waived their right to a jury trial.[8] The defendant, however, has the right to remove the case to a state circuit court.[9] The Act also states that all actions heard in the cybercourt can be conducted by means of 'electronic communications', which include, but are not limited to, 'video and audio conferencing and internet conferencing among the judge and court personnel, parties, witnesses, and other persons necessary to the proceeding'.[10] Although the judge might still hear the case in a courtroom – like space for appearance's sake – witnesses, litigations and lawyers can participate from their offices. The public can observe online the cybercourt's proceedings.[11]

In September 2007 the office of public information in the Michigan Supreme Court stated in a release that 'electronic filing of court documents, known as e-filing, would be permitted in state courts under a package of proposed rules'.[12] The proposal (ADM 2007-12) suggested revising court rules 'for service and filing of court documents so that parties in a case can agree to exchange documents via e-mail'.[13] This shows the progression of using electronic communications in dispute resolutions.

As discussed earlier, there are several countries launching cybercourts, for example Australia, whose Federal Court has founded the Australian eCourt. Different national cybercourts certainly have different standards or procedures. At present, a cybercourt can be located in a specific tangible building, like for instance the Michigan cybercourt situated in the premises of the Michigan Court. However, in the future, where there is likely to be an increased demand for e-courts, to avoid being short of facilities or qualified staff in one specific location, and for the sake of convenience and efficiency, e-courts might eventually have venues in various places. To overcome those barriers, in the author's opinion, an international cybercourt system should be introduced, with uniform online litigation proceedings. It would in particular be suitable for disputes involving an international element in cyberspace.

The 'International Cybercourt of Justice' or 'International Cybercourt Central'[14] could be regarded as a full-scale cybercourt, which would benefit participating countries immensely, because it would eliminate problems concerning recognition of foreign judgments. Participating nations would gain the benefit of enforcing cyber laws against foreign individuals in return for agreeing to recognise the international court's judgments against their own citizens.[15]

Any number of consenting countries could create a cybercourt central pursuant to a treaty, convention or any other agreement, similar to the creation of the International Court of Justice, the European Court of Justice or the European Court of Human Rights.[16] The aim should be to create a dispute resolution forum that is just, fair, impartial, convenient, practical and economical for all parties concerned.[17]

The Cyber Court Central Agreement would contain basic terms and provisions including:

> (1) duties and responsibilities of the parties; (2) user conduct whereby the disputing parties would agree not to use Cybercourt Central to harass or defame others or otherwise use Cybercourt Central for any unlawful purpose; (3) privacy provisions whereby Cybercourt Central would maintain the confidentiality of each cybercase file and allow access to it only those who have a user ID and password; (4) indemnification to the court for any technological malfunction during an electronic filing or loss of confidential material in the cybercase file; and (5) choice of law provisions.[18]

The currently debated issue is how much electronic communication must be used to constitute a cybercourt? It is hard to calculate time, quantity and frequency with electronic communication. But it should at least be clear that the basic amount of electronic communication used in cybercourts would necessitate the creation of the disputants' electronic IDs, submission of case e-documents or e-evidence through a secure database, e-court procedures, hearings and production of court judgments electronically.

On the basis of the Michigan Cybercourt's experience, although courts have the advantage of publicity and accountability, some other fundamental issues of cybercourts, which are similar to basic elements of the entire ODR system, need to be discussed such as functional equivalence of e-documents and e-evidence, jurisdiction, choice of law, enforceability of judgments and choice of court.

4.2 Electronic ADR services

There are three successful experiences of e-ADR services:

- ICANN (the Internet Corporation for Assigned Names and Numbers) and WIPO-UDRP (the World Intellectual Property Organization Uniform Domain Name Dispute Resolution Policy);
- e-Bay and SquareTrade;
- AAA and Cybersettle.

4.2.1 ICANN and WIPO-UDRP

Based in Geneva and Switzerland, the WIPO Arbitration and Mediation Centre was established in 1994. It provides ADR services, in particular arbitration and mediation, for the resolution of international commercial disputes between private parties. The WIPO Electronic Case Facility developed by the Centre aims to offer time and cost efficient arbitration and mediation in cross-border dispute settlement.[19]

With the rapid growth of internet users together with increasing cross-border domain name disputes, ICANN – the organisation responsible for managing the generic top level domains – was in urgent need of a solution to the dispute resolution problem.[20] WIPO, which has conducted extensive consultations with members of the internet community around the world, prepared and published a report containing recommendations dealing with domain name issues. Based on the report's recommendations, ICANN adopted the Uniform Domain Name Dispute Resolution Policy (UDRP), which came into effect on 1 December 1999 for all ICANN-accredited registrars of internet domain names. WIPO is accredited by ICANN as a domain name dispute resolution service provider.[21]

Scholars identify the following six specific reasons for the success of UDRP:[22]

1. The participation of WIPO adds *credibility* to the process.
2. The procedure is *transparent*: decisions are available online immediately in full text.
3. The procedure is *self-executing*: two months after filing, the case is closed. Foreign authorities cannot block the outcome.
4. The procedure is *compulsory*: the UDRP clause is imposed on every dot.com registrant. Trademark owners can force registrants to undergo the procedure.
5. The subject matter of domain names is publicity sensitive, and thus attracts press interest, which imposes a degree of public *accountability*.
6. The procedure is *efficient*: all interaction is electronic. This forces people to deal with the matter by electronic means solely, quickly and efficiently.

4.2.2 e-Bay and SquareTrade

A second example of a successful ADR service is e-Bay's e-trust strategy: in order to attract a maximum number of sellers and buyers to the marketplace, e-Bay is engaged in making customers comfortable in buying and selling on e-Bay through a variety of trust building measures like the mutual rating system, which allows for online reputation, identity verification, secure online payment services like PayPal or Escrow, insurance, and last but not least the ODR service of SquareTrade.[23]

SquareTrade is an independent private ODR provider established in 1999. It views its role as establishing trust in online transactions by providing an effective means for the resolution of individual disputes. It deals with 'dispute[s] involving non-delivery of goods or services, misrepresentation, improper selling practices, un-honoured guarantees or warranties, unsatisfactory services, credit and billing problems, unfulfilled contracts, etc.'.[24] The general operation of the e-Bay–SquareTrade dispute resolution system is:

- to provide an automated negotiation platform, offered to e-Bay members free of charge;[25]
- to refer those disputes not resolved through automated negotiation to online mediation, offered by SquareTrade for a nominal sum of fees to e-Bay users.[26]

SquareTrade not only offers dispute resolution services to e-Bay users, but also provides trust seals or 'Seal Membership'.[27] The seal, to an even greater extent than SquareTrade's dispute resolution services, is a distinctive e-Bay service. Under this system, SquareTrade verifies the identity and address of e-Bay sellers, who in return commit to a specified set of selling standards and pay a low fee to SquareTrade. The seal is an icon that is displayed by the seller's ID on e-Bay but remains under the complete control of SquareTrade. SquareTrade can follow trends on buyers' activities and habits since these patterns are recorded when buyers click on the seal. It can also remove the seal icon at any time should a seller no longer meet the requirements.[28]

Most importantly, the SquareTrade experience points to new possibilities for addressing one of the most difficult problems in the mediation world – the accountability dilemma. This dilemma stems from the fact that accountability hinges on transparency and structure, while mediation's strength is drawn, to a large extent, from its confidentiality and flexibility.[29] An essential component in SquareTrade's accountability system is its substantial database on resolution efforts. SquareTrade has managed to gather extensive information internally without completely foregoing confidentiality externally. SquareTrade collects a vast amount of information on the services it provides, much of which is gathered in real time, simultaneously with the act of participation in the ODR process. The information remains accessible to SquareTrade, the mediator and the parties for up to one year.[30] SquareTrade also collects the other data information in seal application and the user registration form. At the conclusion of the dispute resolution process, SquareTrade records 'Resolution Behaviour Information', which comprises information on whether a party participated in the process to completion, whether an agreement was reached, whether the party accepted or rejected a mediator's recommendation, and whether a respondent had been involved in multiple cases of this type.[31]

Moreover, the typical e-Bay dispute concerns objective technicalities and does not produce tensions and emotions that require a confidential setting for its resolution, as do, for example, disputes involving trade secrets or sexual harassment.[32]

Finally, e-Bay refers its users exclusively to SquareTrade though a link on its website. Thus, SquareTrade's position is practically that of an in-house dispute resolution provider that is embedded in the fabric of the organisation to which it provides its services, and so offers some of the same possibilities but also raises similar concerns.[33] SquareTrade has the advantage of taking a high volume of disputes, thereby revealing any chronic deficiencies in the dispute resolution system itself. It might be necessary to improve its services, by improving incentives for the participation and enforcement of settlements by insisting on disputing parties' long-term interests such as reputation rating, feedback rating and seal membership.[34]

4.2.3 AAA and Cybersettle

On 2 October 2006 the American Arbitration Association (AAA) and Cybersettle, Inc., announced a strategic alliance that will provide clients of both companies with the opportunity to use the dispute resolution services of both companies exclusively. With the goal of 'ensuring that no one walks away without a resolution', AAA clients using the AAA's online case management tools will be able to attempt to settle with Cybersettle before AAA neutrals are selected. And Cybersettle clients who have not been able to reach settlement through online negotiation will be able to switch to the AAA's dispute resolution processes, including conciliation, mediation and arbitration (Figure 4.1).[35]

Figure 4.1 **The AAA and Cybersettle strategic alliance**

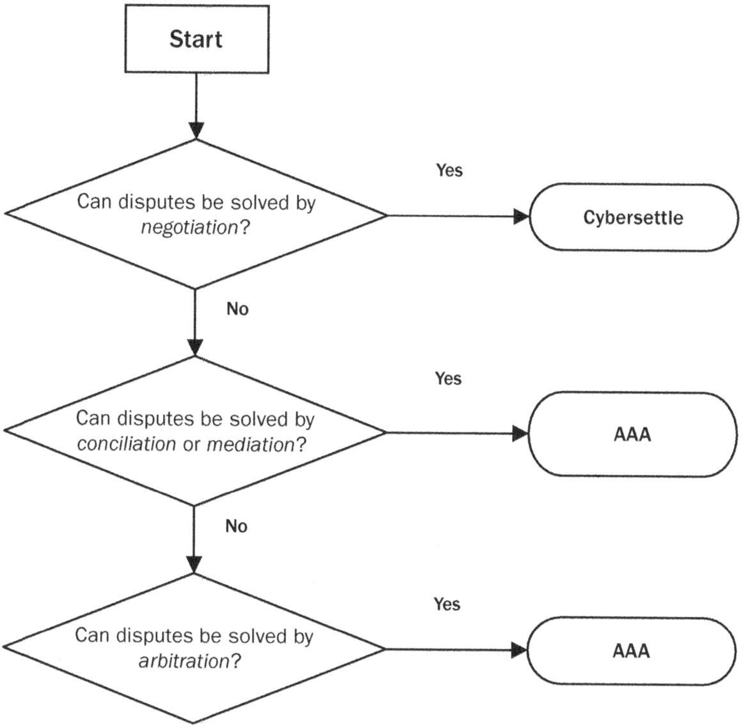

The benefits of the cooperation between AAA and Cybersettle are threefold:

- *Reputation and merits*: The AAA is a non-profit-making public service organisation. It also serves as a centre for education and training, issues specialised publications, and conducts research on all forms of out-of-court dispute settlement. Cybersettle, for instance, a pioneer in online negotiation, is the inventor and patent-holder of the online double-blind bid system.[36]
- *Experiences*: AAA offers a broad range of dispute resolution services to business executives, attorneys, individuals, trade associations, unions, management, consumers, families, communities and all levels of government, while since 1996 Cybersettle has handled more than 162,000 transactions, with more than US$1.2 billion in settlements.[37]
- *Professional regulations*: AAA has commercial arbitration rules and mediation procedures, including procedures for large, complex commercial disputes, as well as supplementary rules for the resolution of patent disputes and a practical guide on drafting dispute resolution clauses, including negotiation, mediation, arbitration and large, complex cases. Cybersettle can contribute its private practices and work with AAA to promote other services when appropriate and to make joint proposals and business presentations under certain circumstances.[38]

When comparing the ICANN–WIPO-UDRP, SquareTrade–e-Bay and AAA–Cybersettle examples, what is striking is that these three ODR service providers do not only make a very attractive offer for easily accessible, quick, effective and low-cost dispute resolution, but most importantly have succeeded in integrating their offer to the primary markets for domain name registration and e-commerce, where online disputes evolve.[39]

This integration is brought about in all these three cases by cooperation agreements with the primary market makers, for example, WIPO-UDRP with ICANN, SquareTrade with e-Bay, and Cybersettle with AAA, and by creating socio-legal bonds for potential dispute parties to commit to the process.[40] That is, the ICANN UDRP administrative procedure is mandatory to domain name holders, while the SquareTrade mediation process is mandatory to e-Bay sellers.

One more additional credential that makes WIPO-UDRP successful is that ICANN with WIPO has a self-enforcement mechanism. The ICANN-accredited registrars reserve the right to transfer or cancel a domain name directly.[41]

But in the future, how can the existing ODR service providers improve? And how can the newly established ones learn from past achievements? To answer this question, we must understand the three fundamental features or building blocks of any ODR system: convenience, trust and expertise (Figure 4.2).[42]

With offline disputes, ODR is likely to surface as an add-on to other already existing processes. There will then be a choice between ODR and ADR processes, and some assessment will have to be made of the relative amount of convenience, trust and expertise provided by each dispute resolution process.[44]

The factors convenience, trust and expertise are generally not independent of each other. In other words, if the level of one factor is changed, the level of some other factor may be affected. Raising one factor a lot may lower another factor a little, often a beneficial trade-off. Or raising one factor a lot may, at the same time, also raise the level of some other factor, almost certainly a desirable outcome.[45]

What is challenging is that the impact of making changes in a system will depend on who the parties are and what the context is. There is often a trade-off between the power of an application (expertise) and how complicated it is to use (convenience).[46]

As we can see from Figure 4.3, when the process is fairly high on convenience and expertise, trust, legitimacy and fairness are quite weak.

Figure 4.2 **Three fundamental features of ODR[43]**

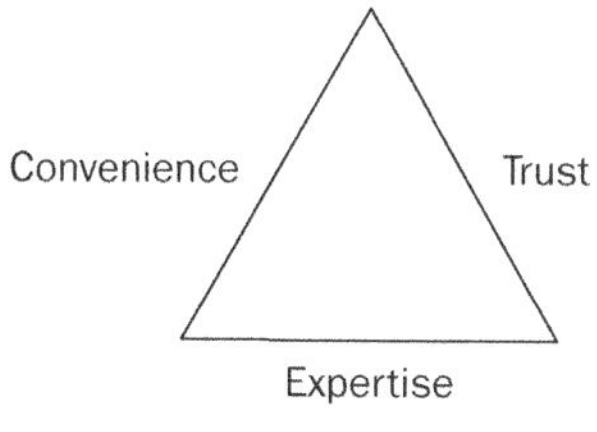

Figure 4.3 **The ICANN-UDRP diagram[47] (left) and the SmartSettle negotiation diagram[48] (right)**

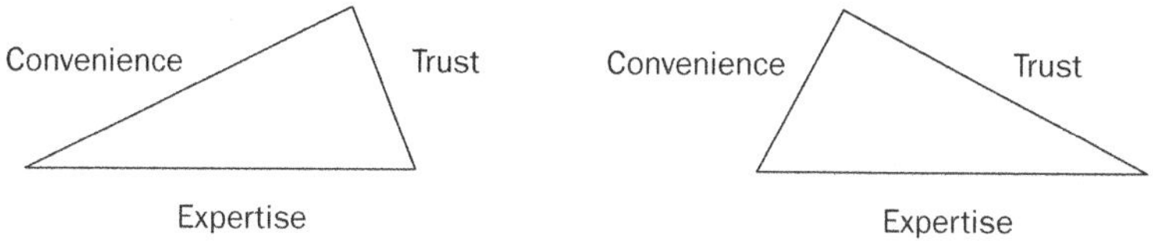

On the other hand, where expertise and trust levels are very high, convenience is low. It is possible that when a process is short of expertise, parties' convenience increases together with trust because of self-command, for example in blind bidding systems.

Therefore, in the future, ODR service providers should consider the balance of the three elements in order to gain success.

Notes

1. Michigan Supreme Court, Annual Report 2001, available at http://courts.michigan.gov/scao/resources/publications/statistics/2001execsum.pdf (accessed 28 May 2008).
2. Schultz (2004), pp. 71, 104.
3. Michigan Supreme Court, Annual Report 2001.
4. Michigan Cybercourt, available at http://michigancybercourt.net/Documents/court-docs.htm (accessed 29 Nov 2006).
5. Ponte and Cavenagh (2005), p. 110.
6. 2001 Michigan Public Acts 262, 8005, available at http://www.michiganlegislature.org/mileg.asp?page=getObject&objName=2001-HB-4140&userid= (accessed 29 Nov 2006).
7. Michigan Public Act 262 of 2001, 8003.
8. Ibid., 8009.
9. Ibid., 8007(1).
10. Ibid., 8011.
11. Ponte and Cavenagh (2005), p. 111.
12. For Immediate Release Electronic Filing Rules on Agenda for Michigan Supreme Court Pubic Hearing, available at http://courts.michigan.gov/supremecourt/Press/publichearing92607.pdf (accessed 28 May 2008).
13. Ibid.
14. Exon (2002), pp. 1, 5.
15. Windham (2005), pp. 1, 5.
16. Perritt (1998), pp. 1121, 1147.
17. Exon (2002), pp. 1, 36.
18. Ibid., pp. 1, 12.
19. The WIPO Arbitration and Mediation Centre, available at http://www.wipo.int/amc/en/index.html (accessed 29 May 2008).
20. See http://www.icann.org/ (accessed 29 May 2008).
21. See Frequently Asked Questions: Internet Domain Names at http://www.wipo.int/amc/en/center/faq/domains.html (accessed 29 May 2008).
22. Motion (2005), pp. 137–69, see also UDRP official documents available at http://www.icann.org/udrp/ (accessed 3 September 2007).
23. Calliess (2006), pp. 647, 652.
24. See http://www.squaretrade.com (accessed 29 November 2006).
25. Rabinovich-Einy (2006), pp. 253, 258.
26. Ibid, pp. 253, 259.

27. See http://www.squaretrade.com (accessed 29 November 2006).
28. Rabinovich-Einy (2006), pp. 253, 259.
29. Ibid., p. 256.
30. Ibid., p. 270.
31. For the SquareTrade privacy policy, see http://www.squaretrade.com/cnt/jsp/lgl/user_conf_agree.jsp?vhostid=chipotle&stmp=squaretradeconf_infocollect (accessed 29 November 2006).
32. See http://www.squaretrade.com (accessed 29 November 2006).
33. Rabinovich-Einy (2006), pp. 253, 278.
34. Ibid., pp. 279–81.
35. AAA (n.d.).
36. See http://www.adr.org (accessed 14 December 2006).
37. See http://www.adr.org/sp.asp?id=28818 (accessed 14 December 2006).
38. See http://www.adr.org (accessed 14 December 2006).
39. Calliess (2006), pp. 647, 653.
40. From my perspective, 'social-legal bones' means the combination of the powers between social organisations and legislation. The term 'legal bond' is being used in a very broad sense, including not only contractual design but also all kinds of 'private ordering'; see more details in http://odrworkshop.info/papers2005/odrworkshop2005Bol.pdf.
41. See http://www.icann.org/tlds/agreements/name/registry-agmt-appl-03jul01.htm (accessed 3 September 2007).
42. Katsh and Rifkin (2001), p. 73.
43. Ibid., p. 75.
44. Ibid.
45. Ibid., p. 76.
46. Ibid.
47. Ibid.
48. Ibid., p. 77.

5

The future of ODR

ODR has become more and more popular in resolving cross-border disputes. There is a need to have internationally uniform and mandatory rules or procedures to resolve disputes online, as the quality of services provided by ODR service providers will heavily affect ODR users' confidence and influence future trends on ODR development. In the author's opinion, the major issues that must be resolved to regulate the ODR market and strengthen ODR use are to experiment and clarify core principles of ODR service standards and to recommend a model for codes of conduct or practice for ODR service providers.

5.1 Core principles

5.1.1 Accountability (transparency) v. confidentiality

Accountability means being answerable to an authority that can mandate desirable conduct and sanction conduct that breaches identified obligations.[1] Accountability mechanisms fall into two categories: one is structure and the other is transparency. Accountability can be internal and external, or both. Internal accountability typically promotes self-evaluation and organisational development and enhances management practices and strategic planning through internal measures and review,[2] while external accountability usually involves evaluation of performance and outcomes by a credible external entity (private or public) in the context of predetermined boundaries.[3]

Transparency is one of the strongest elements to induce trust in using ODR, because it provides information for ODR users to determine whether the ODR provider is trustworthy, whether effective redress mechanisms are available, whether the cost and duration is reasonable and whether it is suitable for their nature of disputes.

According to the above functions, transparency should be related to three categories: disclosure of ODR providers, including ownership and location of the provider; disclosure of ODR process, including duration and costs, the character of the outcome (binding or non-binding), and substantive rules or principles governing the merits; and disclosure of neutrals.[4] The publication of the results of ODR proceedings in particular seems to be essential for inducing trust in ODR. If one cannot know what results these proceedings produce, one would find it very hard to assess and thus trust them.[5]

On the other hand, confidentiality is another legitimate concern in ODR procedures – that the information of disputants and information gathered during the proceeding will not be disclosed, and the results of the cases will not be published, unless permission is given to do so. Confidentiality creates a safe haven for disputants, allowing them to bring forth disputes that they may not have been willing to pursue through formal, public avenues on one hand, but confidentiality protection of ODR proceedings may reduce the general public's trust in the process and deter future disputants from using it on the other.[6]

ODR providers have to strike a balance between the privacy desired by the parties using these techniques, and the transparency, accountability and building of trust, which is engendered by publishing the decisions of the ODR provider.[7] So what are the solutions to accommodate these two conflicting needs: transparency v. confidentiality?

To the author's knowledge, confidentiality is more sensitive in B2B than B2C matters, generally because the former may involve higher financial stakes as well as a certain level of technique and strategies of business. Therefore, the disclosure of B2B ODR outcomes may affect the reputation of a business and the confidentiality of trade secrets. In principle, information about ODR proceedings and outcomes, which reaches a minimum amount of money and which is deemed to be related to any trade secrets and personal sensitive issues, must be kept confidential, except for the pre-agreements. However, in order to increase trust in their ODR services, ODR providers can still allow the disclosure of those outcomes, when agreed by users, or when beyond the conditions of confidential protection. In addition, ODR providers can report some statistics showing the percentage of dispute settlements, as well as the rate of settlement satisfaction. However, this must be assessed by authorised bodies, such as accreditation agencies. The end of this section considers such mechanisms and their functions.

With regard to small and medium-sized entrepreneurs (SMEs), effective structural accountability should be introduced to reconcile confidentiality on one hand with accountability on the other. Effective structural accountability incorporates both internal and external elements. Internally, goals are defined and targets are set, processes for measuring and monitoring performance are instituted, and improvement is sought. Externally, beyond setting the general framework, particular goals and performance evaluation are audited and questioned in an additional effort to detect and remedy poor performance, misconduct, inefficiencies and deficient policies.[8]

According to the previous analysis of SquareTrade's successful experience, SquareTrade has generated internal accountability by instituting structures for:

- gathering broad and rich information on interventions by neutrals and party needs as well as ongoing efforts to evaluate the quality of services rendered;
- monitoring neutrals performance;
- developing the standard of confidentiality;
- internalising incentives for neutrals to perform well and for the system as a whole to identify deficiencies and successes and learn from them.[9]

SquareTrade's efforts are mainly internal. It still needs to work on external accountability such as oversight by a credible, independent entity. External accountability is important to ODR providers because it can assist them in questioning the adequacy of the goals themselves and the means used to achieve them, drawing on the information revealed in the course of monitoring as well as their own experience and knowledge from other settings, revealing those instances of poor performance missed in the internal examination, and providing an impartial evaluation of potential conflicts of interests between providers.[10] After all, external accountability can be gained by accreditation.

5.1.2 Accessibility

According to the ICC, accessibility means 'all relevant correspondence relating to a transaction should be easily accessible and made available to the customer upon request'.[11] It is suggested that the ODR system should always be available to users to give them access to the process and to their own cases except during scheduled downtime.[12] In the author's view, to increase accessibility, the ODR service providers should be reliable for the users to access and review the dispute resolution service clauses. Such clauses should appear automatically on the screen or be accessed by clicking a link.

5.1.3 Credibility and accreditation

Accreditation is deemed to be a precondition for practitioners to practise, involving a practitioner meeting certain levels of education, training or performance.[13] In the US the Association for Conflict Resolution (ACR) and the ABA have each developed task forces on promoting mediation certification to overcome the lack of uniformity in the various mediation practice codes since 2002.[14] However, the Mediator Certification Program has not been progressing due to the result of the 'Mediator Certification Feasibility Studytudy'.[15]

Australia is another pioneering country to have a strongly recommended and developed accreditation system for ADR practitioners. In August 2004, the Australian National Alternative Dispute Resolution Advisory Council (NADRAC) took an initiative on mediator accreditation released in two working papers: 'Who Says You're a Mediator?'[16] and 'Who Can Refer To, or Conduct, Mediation?'[17] In 2006, at the 8th National Mediation Conference in Hobart, the Draft National Mediation Accreditation System was approved. The Committee strongly recommended moving the scheme to an implementation phase reported in 'Mediation Accreditation in Australia'.[18] On 1 January 2008 the new National Mediator Accreditation System implemented uniform standards in accrediting mediators.

Meanwhile, a new National Mediator Accreditation Committee is being established to implement the National Mediator Accreditation System. It will be responsible for developing and reviewing the operation of the standards, developing a national register of accredited mediators, monitoring, auditing and supporting complaints-handling processes and promoting mediation.[19] The NADRAC previously reported that 'a major difficulty for policy-makers in relation to accreditation has been the absence of a nationally co-ordinated approach to the accreditation of ADR practitioners'.[20] Therefore, it is suggested that establishing minimum standards for ADR practitioners and mechanisms for selecting those practitioners are important for an ADR system.[21] In September 2007 the Approval Standards of Australian National Mediator

Standards for Mediators Seeking Approval Under the National Mediator Accreditation System recommended that to be accredited, the Recognised Mediation Accreditation Body (RMAB) requires a mediator to provide evidence of good character, relevant insurance, employee status, education, training and experience and so on, as well as to meet the threshold approval requirements and ongoing professional education requirements.[22]

In order to practice ODR, a practitioner must also be accredited to meet certain levels of education, training and performance.[23] Accreditation will bring credibility to ODR by ensuring that the practice of ODR is built on a foundation of quality assurance.[24] Accreditation can be imposed by ODR service providers or by government and international organisations.

ODR has grown out of the history of offline ADR and many standards or requirements of an ADR system can be reflected in the criteria for accreditation in ODR; however, ODR practitioners still need to meet a minimum level of knowledge and possess familiarity with specific skills, in particular, knowledge of ODR software systems and training of computer and IT skills. In 2002 the NADRAC recommended knowledge areas for online practitioners including online cultures, online technology, online communication, online negotiation processes, online context, online procedures and online decision-making.[25] Furthermore, it suggested that ODR practitioners should be able to access a dispute for ODR, gather and use information online, define the dispute online, manage the online process and interaction between parties, and conclude the ODR process.[26]

There are at least four distinct models for accreditation of ADR practitioners as identified by the ABA in 2002.[27] It proposed that accreditation systems can be characterised according to the 'hurdles' they set for initial selection of practitioners and the 'maintenance' procedures for ensuring quality practice:

- low hurdles with low maintenance;
- low hurdles with high maintenance;
- high hurdles with low maintenance;
- high hurdles with high maintenance.

Arguably, each of the above four models could be appropriate in different situations depending on factors such as the client group, the level of acceptance of ODR, and the maturity of ODR practice.[28] The ABA found that the majority of accreditation systems within the US currently have fairly low hurdles and maintenance,[29] while SquareTrade provides higher hurdles and maintenance.[30] The author believes that high hurdles and maintenance will be the direction for the success of future ODR services, because it will reduce practitioner diversity, improve practitioner skills, increase public credibility and ensure quality practice.

The criteria for accreditation in ODR include mainly practitioner knowledge, such as technology and language, and practitioner skills, such as maintaining communication and controlling information flow. The standard can be achieved by:

- incorporating ODR into current practitioner accreditation systems;
- independently accrediting ODR practitioners;
- accrediting specialist ODR skills;
- accrediting agencies providing ODR.[31]

In the author's opinion, ODR is new and challenging not only for individuals but also for agencies, so accreditation systems should consider accrediting both agencies and individuals at the same time. If the ODR service providers employ a ranking system so users can grade their ODR practioners according to the level of service they provide, it will boost confidence among potential ODR users and improve the quality of ODR services. In addition, the international organisations such as the UNCITRAL should work closely with the ABA and NADRAC to provide ODR accreditation and produce a model law on international accreditation of ODR practitioners.

5.1.4 Security

Security is another core issue in ODR because it is concerned not only with a disputant's identity but also with the protection of confidential information. In the online environment, the identity of a person in a dispute is not always clear. How can one be sure that the person one is dealing with is who he claims to be? Moreover, ODR providers state that the information collected is treated confidentially, but does this necessarily mean that such information cannot be transmitted or accessed additionally?

Under these circumstances, safeguards have emerged, including the development of digital signatures, which provide authentication, integrity of a message, and non-reputation of sending and trust marks.

In the author's opinion, digital signatures must be mandatory to the protection of e-mails and web-based communications. Standard e-mails such as those provided for free cannot guarantee the requirements of the protection of the confidentiality and integrity of the information, thus e-mails in ODR must be secured by a digital signature, or its equivalent, such as the Secure Multipurpose Internet Mail Exchange Protocol (S/MIME) or the Pretty Good Privacy program.

Furthermore, specific means of protection must also be used when confidential information is communicated over the internet, the most common being the Transport Layer Security (TLS), the successor to the Secure Sockets Layer (SSL) protocol. They are very similar cryptographic tools, which provide secure communications across the internet protecting the confidentiality and integrity of data transmissions. These protocols also allow most types of application (such as web browsing, e-mail, instant messaging, video conferencing and other data transfers) to communicate across networks in a way designed to prevent tampering or forgery.

Video conferencing, used in the course of ODR, is a tool that enables face-to-face, real-time communications between people around the world. During a video or audio conference, sensitive information and data can be communicated across internal and external networks where it is susceptible to hackers. Therefore, conferencing must have security protocols in place for data storage and data transmission. The main reason for this is because conferences are often archived for future use. As the information discussed could be sensitive, data storage needs to be secure and separate from internal networks. Today, most companies subscribe to video conferencing services that store data in special offsite facilities. The level of encryption depends on the sensitivity of the data. Thus, ODR providers must offer a provision of security in the user agreement. Take SquareTrade as an example: an e-signatures and writings clause specifies that 'you acknowledge and agree that the standards of the Uniform Electronic Transactions Act, adopted in 1999 and applied in the State California'. At the international and national level there is also other e-signatures legislation, which can be used for ODR service agreements.

5.1.5 Enforceability

The enforcement in court of mediation and negotiation outcomes, on the one hand, and of arbitral awards, on the other hand, follows

> different procedures. In a nutshell, one may say that the enforcement of the former requires an ordinary court action, whilst the enforcement of the latter can be granted in summary proceedings without a review of the merits of the award.[32]

As ODR is just an electronic version of traditional negotiation, mediation, arbitration and court litigation, the enforceability of an ODR clause in the contract should be examined according to the enforceability of traditional offline dispute resolution clauses. However, difficulties may arise as ODR is just an electronic means or platform that parties choose, thus parties might not always indicate a specific procedure, such as e-negotiation, e-mediation, e-arbitration or e-court. If parties include a clause of arbitration through ODR, whether courts will enforce such an agreement to arbitrate is a crucial issue. Or if parties include a mediation clause, how can they seek enforcement afterwards? We will discuss the solutions below.

Settlement agreements

A settlement agreement is a contract; it does not have the binding force of a judgment.[33] Thus, it must be enforced by bringing a contract action in court, obtaining a judgment, and possibly starting enforcement of judgment proceedings.[34] For example, mediation and non-binding arbitration outcomes are generally regarded as settlement agreements, whose main issue is the consequence on the ensuing court action of a failure to resort to such a clause.[35] The most recent piece of EU legislation is in support of enforceability of settlement agreements. Article 6 (1) of the Mediation Directive (see Appendix B) provides that member states shall make sure of the possible enforceability of a written agreement resulting from mediation.[36] It is provided that the enforcement can be made through a court or other competent authority in a judgment or decision or in an authentic instrument in accordance with the law of the member state.[37]

So which court will enforce the settlement agreement? The Hague Convention on Choice of Court Agreement in 2005 is the litigation equivalent of the New York Convention because it seeks to provide an equal and viable alternative to arbitration.[38] From the US perspective, though choice-of-court agreements are generally recognised at the federal level, but not clear at the state level, there is a need for an international convention on choice of court. In the EU, under its Article 26, the Choice of Court Convention will trump the Brussels I

Regulation[39] when one party is resident outside the EU, even if the court selected is within the EU. In this case, the Brussels I Regulation 'disconnects' and the Choice of Court Convention controls.[40] It is in favour of a court in both member states and non-member states. The aims of the Choice of Court Convention are to facilitate dispute resolutions and it therefore makes litigation a more viable alternative to arbitration because it ensures the enforcement of the forum selection clauses just like the New York Convention guarantees the enforcement of arbitration clauses.[41]

However, it is a long road to bring ODR settlement agreements in court. It is submitted that ways of simple enforcement should be strongly recommended. For example, if the settlement is reached in a cybercourt, it will then constitute a judicial settlement, which is similar to the enforcement of judgments according to Article 58 of the Brussels I Regulation.

Furthermore, the enforcement of ODR outcomes may be expressed as extra-judicial settlements in the form of authentic instruments[42] in accordance with Article 57 (1) of the Brussels I Regulation, which states: 'A document which has been formally drawn up or registered as an authentic instrument and is enforceable in one Member State shall, in another Member State, be declared enforceable there...' Articles 57 (2) and (3) continue: 'Arrangements relating to maintenance obligations concluded with administrative authorities or authenticated by them shall also be regarded as authentic instruments... The instrument produced must satisfy the conditions necessary to establish its authenticity in the Member State of origin.'

As discussed above, the enforcement of ODR as a form of authentic instrument requires three conditions to be fulfilled: that the instrument's authenticity is established by a public authority; that the authenticity is not only related to the signature but also to the content of the instrument; and that the instrument can be enforced in the state from which it originates. Out-of-court mediation settlement agreements, drafted instruments from a public notary and state-accredited mediation authority mediated settlements can all be deemed to be authentic instruments.[43]

A third solution may be that settlements take the form of consent awards.[44] It is suggested that the parties to mediation 'conditionally vest the mediator with the additional mantle of arbitrator, with the result that, if an agreement is reached, the mediator can render an arbitral award embodying the parties' agreement'.[45] Alternatively, the parties to a mediation or negotiation insert into the settlement agreement an arbitration clause pursuant to which, in the event of non-performance of the settlement, an arbitrator shall have jurisdiction to turn the settlement into a consent award.[46]

Arbitral awards

There are no uniform definitions of arbitration and arbitral awards in national laws and international instruments. Kaufmann-Kohler and Schultz conclude that 'it is only if the parties intend a decision to be binding like a judgment that it constitutes an award and the process an arbitration'.[47] So how can one recognise and enforce an arbitral award, particularly a foreign award?

This is the last but one of the most complicated obstacles. In most cases, the place of arbitration determines the nationality of an arbitral award. An arbitral award is deemed to be made at the place of arbitration and will have the nationality of the country in which the place of arbitration is situated. Generally, the parties can choose the place of arbitration; when no choice has been expressed by the parties, the arbitrator will determine it. However, it is not absolutely necessary for the relevant matters of the arbitration proceedings to be actually conducted in the territory of the country at the place of arbitration, although the parties may have agreed on the place of arbitration. According to 'the seat theory', which has been recognised and popularly adopted in the national arbitration laws and practices, the relevant matters of the arbitration procedures such as oral hearings and private deliberations of the arbitral tribunal over the case may be concluded in a country other than the place of arbitration, yet the place of arbitration remains unchanged, which is the place of arbitration agreed by the parties.[48]

Under most national arbitration laws, arbitral awards are treated as the domestic awards of the nation where the awards are made. The enforcement of foreign awards is more complicated than that of domestic ones, and is generally regulated by international treaties. The current recognition and enforcement of foreign awards is mainly regulated by the 1958 New York Convention. The key issue is whether the online arbitral awards can be recognised and enforced under the New York Convention internationally. The biggest obstacle in international recognition and enforcement of online arbitral awards according to the New York Convention is whether the awards in digital form meet the requirements on the written form and originals of awards under the Convention, as well as how to solve the signature problem of such awards, because the New York Convention obliges contracting states to enforce an 'agreement in writing' in which parties agree to arbitrate.[49]

Before the international community admits that digital online arbitral awards meet the written form and original requirements of awards under the Convention, and clearly recognises the validity of digital signature by extensive interpretation of the Convention under the principle of functional equivalency, online arbitral awards may still be recognised and enforced internationally according to the New York Convention after being printed out and signed by arbitrators.[50] However, UNCITRAL currently is considering how to update the New York Convention (and the UNCITRAL Model Law on International Arbitration) to deal with electronic documents.[51] In addition, the word 'contract' mentioned in the UN Convention on the Use of Electronic Communications in International Contracts is used in a broad way and covers, for example, arbitration agreements and other legally binding agreements whether or not they are usually called 'contracts'.[52] If so, digital arbitration agreements are automatically recognised under the UN Convention. Furthermore, Article 9(4) of the UN Convention provides a new rule for the electronic functional equivalent of an original document.

The Working Group had initially included a provision on the electronic functional equivalent of an original in order to cover electronic arbitration agreements under the New York Convention ('the Convention on the Recognition and Enforcement of Foreign Arbitral Awards').[53] Article 20 of the UN Convention provides that 'the provision of this Convention apply to the use of electronic communications in connection with the formation or performance of a contract to which any of the following international conventions, to which a Contracting State to this Convention is or may become a Contracting State, apply: "Convention on the Recognition and Enforcement of Foreign Arbitral Awards (New York, 10 June 1958)"'.[54]

Self-enforcement mechanisms

Self-enforcement is also called 'self-execution'. It generates the merits of ODR, low costs and convenience. Self-enforcement can be divided into two categories: direct self-enforcement and indirect self-enforcement.[55] Direct self-enforcement is identical to the ICANN UDRP domain name transfers, which consist in setting up mechanisms controlling the resources at play. However, in enforcing contractual dispute settlements, such mechanisms can be the payment system Escrow, a refund system, a transaction insurance system and technological constraints.[56] In indirect self-enforcement, incentives are created for the losing party to comply voluntarily, for example through the use of trustmarks, reputation management and rating systems, publicly accessible reports, exclusion of participants from marketplaces, and payments for delay in performance.[57]

5.2 Jurisdiction and choice of law clause

If ODR providers breach service agreements with disputing parties, for example, when disclosing confidential information, which court will have jurisdiction? An example is if the disputing Party A is from England, the disputing Party B from China, and the ODR provider from California, USA. Generally, most ODR service agreements have a jurisdiction clause, but if there is no such a clause, how can one determine it?

In the author's opinion, party autonomy should be applied to ODR service agreements. Parties should be free to choose jurisdiction in ODR service contracts. In the case that parties fail to have a jurisdiction clause, it is suggested that the location should be the place of ODR providers' business, in accordance with Article 6 of the UN Convention on the Use of Electronic Communications in International Contracts, which states that 'the place of business is that which has the closest relationship to the relevant contract'. It is sensible that the place of ODR service providers should have the closest relationship to the service agreements. However, Article 6 of the UN Convention further indicates that the location will not necessarily be the place of business merely because (a) the equipment and technology are located; and (b) if the information system may be accessed by other parties. Thus, the place of ODR service providers should be the place where ODR services are registered, but not merely where the equipment and technology are located.

As to the choice of law, party autonomy is a core principle. In the absence of substantive international ODR regulation, parties still need to make a choice between the possible alternatives, such as the UNCITRAL Model Law on E-Commerce, the UNCITRAL Model Law on Electronic Signatures, the UN Convention on the Use of Electronic Communications of International Contracts, the UNCITRAL Model Law on International Commercial Arbitration, the New York Convention, or other national laws. As to online arbitration, in most countries, the law governing arbitration is the law of the place or seat of arbitration. Hence, determining the applicable law requires determining the place of arbitration.[58]

5.3 Model of codes of conduct

The model for codes of conduct should suggest principles for managing ODR, not only with policies but also through methodologies and technologies. In the author's opinion, the proposed model of codes of conduct for handling online disputes should include at least four main provisions:

- *General provisions*: The model should include procedure or formalisation and control mechanisms of the ODR system and its service. It should cover ODR core principles: accountability, transparency, confidentiality, accessibility and security. Moreover, both duty and liability of ODR practitioners should be considered.
- *Specific provisions*: The model should contain specific rules regulating cybercourts or the e-court. It should specify procedures and requirements to use electronic filing, online jury proceedings and commitments to technology.
- *Accreditation mechanism*: The model should cover the accreditation scheme of ODR practitioners, such as the clearing house[59] or appellate bodies, as well as an ODR trustmark scheme. It should consider areas such as the practitioner's character, knowledge, skills, education, professional training and experience.
- *Enforcement mechanism*: The enforcement of ODR settlement agreements should be regulated, including self-enforcement and enforcement in courts.

Notes

1. Minow (2003), pp. 1229, 1260.
2. See Panel on Accountability and Governance in the Voluntary Sector (1999).
3. Hayllar (2000), pp. 60, 68, cited in Rabinovich-Einy (2006), pp. 253, 261.
4. Kaufmann-Kohler and Schultz (2004), p. 110. The term 'neutrals' in this chapter means the third parties, including mediators and arbitrators.
5. Schulze et al. (2001), p. 39.
6. Uniform Mediation Act 2001, prefatory note.

7. Motion (2005), pp. 137–69, 154.
8. Rabinovich-Einy (2006), pp. 253, 269.
9. Ibid., p. 282.
10. Ibid., pp. 282–3.
11. ICC (2003b), p. 9.
12. Ibid., p. 12.
13. Tyler and Bornstein (2006), p. 383.
14. ACR (2004); ABA (2002a).
15. Mediator Certification Feasibility Study, available at http://www.acrnet.org/pdfs/certificationresults2005.pdf (accessed 30 May 2008).
16. NADRAC (2004b).
17. NADRAC (2004a).
18. National Accreditation Standards for Mediators, the 8th Australian National Mediation Conference, available at http://www.mediationconference.com.au/html/implementation.html (accessed 29 May 2008).
19. National Mediator Accreditation System, available at http://www.nadrac.gov.au/agd/WWW/disputeresolutionHome.nsf/Page/Standards_Further_details_about_the_Committee_Meeting (accessed 29 May 2008).
20. NADRAC (2006), pp. 9–10.
21. Ibid., Appendix 3.
22. The Approval Standards of Australian National Mediator Standards for Mediators Seeking Approval Under the National Mediator Accreditation System, September 2007, NADRAC National Mediator Accreditation System, available at http://www.wadra.law.ecu.edu.au/pdf/Final%20%20Approval%20Standards_200907.pdf (accessed 29 May 2008).
23. Tyler and Bornstein (2006), 383.
24. Ibid., p. 384.
25. NADRAC (2002).
26. Ibid.
27. ABA (2002a).
28. Tyler and Bornstein (2006), pp. 383, 386.
29. ABA (2002a).
30. Tyler and Bornstein (2006), pp. 383, 388.
31. Ibid., p. 390.
32. Kaufmann-Kohler and Schultz (2004), p. 211.
33. Ibid.
34. ABA (2002b), pp. 35–8.
35. Kaufmann-Kohler and Schultz (2004), p. 135.
36. Directive 2008/52/EC (the Mediation Directive).
37. Directive 2008/52/EC (the Mediation Directive), Article 6(2).
38. Trooboff (2005), 13.
39. EC Council Regulation on Jurisdiction and the Recognition and Enforcement of Judgments in Civil and Commercial Matter ('Brussels I Regulation').
40. Teitz (2005), pp. 543, 556.
41. Ibid., p. 557.
42. Kaufmann-Kohler and Schultz (2004), p. 212.
43. Ibid., p. 213.

44. Ibid., p. 214.
45. ABA (2002b), p. 37.
46. Stipanowich (2001), pp. 831, 903.
47. Kaufmann-Kohler and Schultz (2004), p. 157.
48. Ibid.
49. 1958 New York Convention, Article II (1).
50. Hu (2005), p. 12.
51. Drahozal (2006), pp. 233, 251; see also UN Secretariat (2005), pp. 1–2.
52. Faria (2006), pp. 689, 690.
53. Wei and Suling (2006), pp. 116, 130.
54. UN Convention on the Use of Electronic Communications in International Contracts, Article 20.
55. Kaufmann-Kohler and Schultz (2004), p. 224.
56. Ibid., p. 232.
57. Ibid., pp. 225–7.
58. Ibid., p. 166.
59. 'The network can play the role of a "clearing house". Such a role entails examination of the matter in dispute in order to choose the appropriate or most appropriate ODR provider for the type of dispute considered. The function of a clearing house would be liaising with the users and the ODR providers throughout the whole process,' Philippe (2002).

6

Conclusions and recommendations

As discussed in the above chapters, the ever-increasing number of IT participants has led to an explosion of e-commerce. Buying and selling online has become a common practice without regard to physical boundaries. However, electronic commercial transactions are developing dramatically, along with newly emerging legal challenges, in particular, the legislative challenge of resolving disputes online.

From a legal perspective, electronic commercial transactions are within the scope of traditional commercial law and international trade law, covering a wide range of legal issues. A noticeable difference from traditional commercial transactions, which are usually carried out face to face, is that the majority of transnational electronic transactions involve people who will never physically meet. This changes the essence of trade law in many ways. However, similar to traditional trade law, contract law, jurisdiction, choice of law, security and dispute resolution are key aspects in e-commerce. It is argued that e-commerce does not provide new insights to the operation of traditional laws, such as contract law; instead it adds a new and different layer of communication by electronic means, so it is not necessary to establish a new body of laws governing issues in electronic commercial transactions.[1] The EU, the US and international organisations like UNCITRAL have considered these matters. The Secretary of UNCITRAL, Jernej Sekolec, for example, recently expressed the view that there should not be a new set of e-commerce laws governing international trade,[2] as it would cause confusion and complicate the law unnecessarily.

In the author's opinion, it would indeed cause confusion if there were two sets of national and international trade laws, one for offline and the other for online transactions – it is common to doubt the practicality of such an approach. But fear of facilitating different sets of laws should not become an obstacle to modernising existing laws to adapt to the future development of various high technologies in electronic commercial transactions. From the research in this book, there is strong evidence showing that electronic commercial transactions have unique characteristics. The concept of electronic transactions is the same as that of traditional transactions, but the actual conduct of electronic transactions is fundamentally different.

Electronic transactions can be deemed to be a means of communication from a technological point of view. However, the legal perspective of the operation of electronic transactions should not be ignored. The two dominant factors that could distinguish the legal consequences of electronic transactions from traditional ones are the determination of 'time and place of dispatch and receipt of an electronic communication',[3] and 'the place of business'[4] in cyberspace. When involving digitised goods with delivery online, these two factors, as explained in this book, would lead to different outcomes in relation to ascertaining the rules of electronic offer and acceptance, jurisdiction and applicable law. Traditional contract law and private international law will not be sufficient to govern these issues.

Furthermore, in the author's opinion, e-commerce law has a similar function to traditional commercial law: to encourage transnational trade. Commercial laws are essential for long-term investments.[5] Companies that engage in long-term transactions will be able to prosper because there are legal mechanisms available to enforce non-performed arrangements.[6] Thus, an established e-commerce legal regime would undoubtedly encourage long-term electronic trading.

However, the author also believes that before drafting completely new e-commerce laws, scholars, legislators and practitioners should work closely together to examine whether existing laws can apply to electronic commercial transactions. If they can, a new explanatory note to the existing offline legislation should explain legal matters applying to e-commerce. If they cannot, then two options are available: to insert new provisions of e-commerce into existing laws or to create new sets of e-commerce laws.

So is there a need to establish legislation on ODR separately from ADR rules? If so, does it need legislation or only codes of practice (self-regulation)?

In the author's view, international and national legislative organisations should amend or update the offline ADR rules by recognising electronic means of communication in resolving disputes and incorporating concepts of online dispute resolution. A separate piece of legislation is also necessary for ODR services, as they require specific software or computing technology as well as special skills of ODR practitioners, so the outline of ODR core principles will be different from those of offline ADR. For example, with regard to the requirement of confidentiality or security, offline ADR rules will require individuals, practitioners or agencies not to disclose the information of disputants, any relevant case materials and outcomes. However, online ADR rules will have to set more specific conditions on confidentiality and security, for instance, parties or practitioners have to be trained to use the software safely, protecting online users' IDs and passwords. In addition, the IT system used in resolving disputes online must meet a minimum standard of security. Moreover, the ODR mechanism should be a very useful and efficient solution to resolve cross-border disputes in small claims between parties, and users' confidence in choosing ODR as a dispute settlement channel affects the survival and development of ODR. At the same time, ODR is a new way to build trust in electronic commercial transactions and boost the e-commerce market.

From the discussion of the current developments of ODR in the EU, the US, Singapore, China and Australia, it is clear that the stage has been reached where it is necessary to establish a uniform code of conduct at the international level. As the global virtual world develops and the popularity of electronic transactions increases there is no doubt that in the not so distant future ODR will handle a large number of the disputes. Thus, a model law or international regulation concerning ODR service is crucial in order to boost the confidence of ODR users and encourage the growth of the ODR market.

With the aim of advising ODR practice for private sectors and recommending ODR rules to legislators, this book clarifies the mechanism of ODR in commercial disputes. Four successful examples have been examined – Michigan Cybercourt, ICANN with WIPO-UDRP, e-Bay with SquareTrade, and AAA with Cybersettle – proving that the linking of ODR service providers and primary market makers, as well as the self-enforcement mechanism of resolution outcomes, are key factors for their success. It is recommended that the conduct of ODR should include six core principles: accountability, confidentiality, accessibility, credibility, security and enforceability, which can be divided into four main provisions in the regulation: general provisions, specific provisions, and provisions on accreditation and enforcement. Enforceability should be one of the most essential requirements in ODR services, since its success will encourage electronic traders or businesses to use ODR to resolve their disputes. It should be possible to convert the outcomes of online mediation and negotiation into settlement agreements, while the decisions of online arbitration should constitute arbitral awards.

Otherwise, the ODR service providers should have their own self-enforcement or self-execution mechanisms to enforce contractual dispute settlements.

In order for ODR to meet the needs and goals of the online community effectively, the following main concerns require further research, practice and clarification:

- the adoption of recognised and enforceable international or cross-border quality standards for ODR service providers;[7]
- the examination and amendment of current ethical codes for the applicability to ODR;[8]
- the determination of appropriate enforcement mechanisms for ODR outcomes;[9]
- the further education and awareness raising of online businesses and the public about ODR processes;[10]
- the experimentation and employment of efficient and secured ODR technologies;
- the establishment of trusted third parties to supervise and guarantee the order of ODR business services.

In short, trust is the most important element to bolster e-business confidence in e-transactions and e-dispute resolutions. In this book, we have investigated how to provide a safe ODR environment. I hope and believe that this book, through the understanding and analysis of the definition, practical relations of parties, technology and legal concerns of ODR mechanisms, reveals some potential research trends. At the same time, by examining the ODR legal frontier in different countries, it provides a model of ODR legislation at the international level and contributes to fundamental ideas on e-confidence in general. In the era of the internet, technology is changing quickly, so modernising, harmonising or facilitating electronic commercial law, in particular rules of ODR, should be considered an important approach.

Notes

1. Dalhuisen (2007), p. 254.
2. Sekolec (2007).
3. UN Convention on the Use of Electronic Communications in International Contracts, Article 10.

4. Ibid., Article 6.
5. Sekolec (2007).
6. Ibid.
7. Ponte and Cavenagh (2005), p. 144.
8. Ibid., p. 146.
9. Ibid.
10. Ibid.

Appendix A
Electronic commercial transactions legislation

	EU	US	China	Int'l (UNCITRAL)
Electronic commerce law	EC Directive on Electronic Commerce	Uniform Computer Information Transactions Act and Uniform Electronic Transactions Act	N/A	UNCITRAL Model Law on E-Commerce
Electronic contracting law	N/A	N/A	N/A	UN Convention on the Use of Electronic Communication in International Contracts
Electronic signatures law	EC Directive on E-Signatures	Electronic Signatures in Global and National Commerce Act	The People's Republic of China on Electronic Signatures	UNCITRAL Model Law on E-Signatures
Private international law regarding electronic transactions	Rome I Convention and Brussels I Regulation	Case studies	Civil Law and Criminal Law of the People's Republic of China	N/A

Appendix B
Directive 2008/52/EC of the European Parliament and of the Council of 21 May 2008 on certain aspects of mediation in civil and commercial matters

DIRECTIVE 2008/52/EC OF THE EUROPEAN PARLIAMENT AND OF THE COUNCIL

of 21 May 2008
on certain aspects of mediation in civil and commercial matters

THE EUROPEAN PARLIAMENT AND THE COUNCIL OF THE EUROPEAN UNION,

Having regard to the Treaty establishing the European Community, and in particular Article 61(c) and the second indent of Article 67(5) thereof,

Having regard to the proposal from the Commission,

Having regard to the Opinion of the European Economic and Social Committee,[1]

Acting in accordance with the procedure laid down in Article 251 of the Treaty,[2]

Whereas:

(1) The Community has set itself the objective of maintaining and developing an area of freedom, security and justice, in which the free movement of persons is ensured. To that end, the Community has to adopt, interalia, measures in the field of judicial cooperation in civil matters that are necessary for the proper functioning of the internal market.

(2) The principle of access to justice is fundamental and, with a view to facilitating better access to justice, the European Council at its meeting in Tampere on 15 and 16 October 1999 called for alternative, extra-judicial procedures to be created by the Member States.

(3) In May 2000 the Council adopted Conclusions on alternative methods of settling disputes under civil and commercial law, stating that the establishment of basic principles in this area is an essential step towards enabling the appropriate development and operation of extrajudicial procedures for the settlement of disputes in civil and commercial matters so as to simplify and improve access to justice.

(4) In April 2002 the Commission presented a Green Paper on alternative dispute resolution in civil and commercial law, taking stock of the existing situation as concerns alternative dispute resolution methods in the European Union and initiating widespread consultations with Member States and interested parties on possible measures to promote the use of mediation.

(5) The objective of securing better access to justice, as part of the policy of the European Union to establish an area of freedom, security and justice, should encompass access to judicial as well as extrajudicial dispute resolution methods. This Directive should contribute to the proper functioning of the internal market, in particular as concerns the availability of mediation services.

(6) Mediation can provide a cost-effective and quick extra-judicial resolution of disputes in civil and commercial matters through processes tailored to the needs of the parties. Agreements resulting from mediation are more likely to be complied with voluntarily and are more likely to preserve an amicable and sustainable relationship between the parties. These benefits become even more pronounced in situations displaying cross-border elements.

(7) In order to promote further the use of mediation and ensure that parties having recourse to mediation can rely on a predictable legal

framework, it is necessary to introduce framework legislation addressing, in particular, key aspects of civil procedure.

(8) The provisions of this Directive should apply only to mediation in cross-border disputes, but nothing should prevent Member States from applying such provisions also to internal mediation processes.

(9) This Directive should not in any way prevent the use of modern communication technologies in the mediation process.

(10) This Directive should apply to processes whereby two or more parties to a cross-border dispute attempt by themselves, on a voluntary basis, to reach an amicable agreement on the settlement of their dispute with the assistance of a mediator. It should apply in civil and commercial matters. However, it should not apply to rights and obligations on which the parties are not free to decide themselves under the relevant applicable law. Such rights and obligations are particularly frequent in family law and employment law.

(11) This Directive should not apply to pre-contractual negotiations or to processes of an adjudicatory nature such as certain judicial conciliation schemes, consumer complaint schemes, arbitration and expert determination or to processes administered by persons or bodies issuing a formal recommendation, whether or not it be legally binding as to the resolution of the dispute.

(12) This Directive should apply to cases where a court refers parties to mediation or in which national law prescribes mediation. Furthermore, in so far as a judge may act as a mediator under national law, this Directive should also apply to mediation conducted by a judge who is not responsible for any judicial proceedings relating to the matter or matters in dispute. This Directive should not, however, extend to attempts made by the court or judge seised to settle a dispute in the context of judicial proceedings concerning the dispute in question or to cases in which the court or judge seised requests assistance or advice from a competent person.

(13) The mediation provided for in this Directive should be a voluntary process in the sense that the parties are themselves in charge of the process and may organise it as they wish and terminate it at any time. However, it should be possible under national law for the courts to set time-limits for a mediation process. Moreover, the courts should be able to draw the parties' attention to the possibility of mediation whenever this is appropriate.

(14) Nothing in this Directive should prejudice national legislation making the use of mediation compulsory or subject to incentives or sanctions provided that such legislation does not prevent parties from exercising their right of access to the judicial system. Nor should anything in this Directive prejudice existing self-regulating mediation systems in so far as these deal with aspects which are not covered by this Directive.

(15) In order to provide legal certainty, this Directive should indicate which date should be relevant for determining whether or not a dispute which the parties attempt to settle through mediation is a cross-border dispute. In the absence of a written agreement, the parties should be deemed to agree to use mediation at the point in time when they take specific action to start the mediation process.

(16) To ensure the necessary mutual trust with respect to confidentiality, effect on limitation and prescription periods, and recognition and enforcement of agreements resulting from mediation, Member States should encourage, by any means they consider appropriate, the training of mediators and the introduction of effective quality control mechanisms concerning the provision of mediation services.

(17) Member States should define such mechanisms, which may include having recourse to market-based solutions, and should not be required to provide any funding in that respect. The mechanisms should aim at preserving the flexibility of the mediation process and the autonomy of the parties, and at ensuring that mediation is conducted in an effective, impartial and competent way. Mediators should be made aware of the existence of the European Code of Conduct for Mediators which should also be made available to the general public on the Internet.

(18) In the field of consumer protection, the Commission has adopted a Recommendation[3] establishing minimum quality criteria which out-of-court bodies involved in the consensual resolution of consumer disputes should offer to their users. Any mediators or organisations coming within the scope of that Recommendation should be encouraged to respect its principles. In order to facilitate the dissemination of information concerning such bodies, the Commission should set up a database of out-of-court schemes which Member States consider as respecting the principles of that Recommendation.

(19) Mediation should not be regarded as a poorer alternative to judicial proceedings in the sense that compliance with agreements resulting from mediation would depend on the good will of the parties. Member States should therefore ensure that the parties to a written

agreement resulting from mediation can have the content of their agreement made enforceable. It should only be possible for a Member State to refuse to make an agreement enforceable if the content is contrary to its law, including its private international law, or if its law does not provide for the enforceability of the content of the specific agreement. This could be the case if the obligation specified in the agreement was by its nature unenforceable.

(20) The content of an agreement resulting from mediation which has been made enforceable in a Member State should be recognised and declared enforceable in the other Member States in accordance with applicable Community or national law. This could, for example, be on the basis of Council Regulation (EC) No 44/2001 of 22 December 2000 on jurisdiction and the recognition and enforcement of judgments in civil and commercial matters[4] or Council Regulation (EC) No 2201/2003 of 27 November 2003 concerning jurisdiction and the recognition and enforcement of judgments in matrimonial matters and the matters of parental responsibility.[5]

(21) Regulation (EC) No 2201/2003 specifically provides that, in order to be enforceable in another Member State, agreements between the parties have to be enforceable in the Member State in which they were concluded. Consequently, if the content of an agreement resulting from mediation in a family law matter is not enforceable in the Member State where the agreement was concluded and where the request for enforceability is made, this Directive should not encourage the parties to circumvent the law of that Member State by having their agreement made enforceable in another Member State.

(22) This Directive should not affect the rules in the Member States concerning enforcement of agreements resulting from mediation.

(23) Confidentiality in the mediation process is important and this Directive should therefore provide for a minimum degree of compatibility of civil procedural rules with regard to how to protect the confidentiality of mediation in any subsequent civil and commercial judicial proceedings or arbitration.

(24) In order to encourage the parties to use mediation, Member States should ensure that their rules on limitation and prescription periods do not prevent the parties from going to court or to arbitration if their mediation attempt fails. Member States should make sure that this result is achieved even though this Directive does not harmonise national rules on limitation and prescription periods. Provisions on limitation and prescription periods in international

agreements as implemented in the Member States, for instance in the area of transport law, should not be affected by this Directive.

(25) Member States should encourage the provision of information to the general public on how to contact mediators and organisations providing mediation services. They should also encourage legal practitioners to inform their clients of the possibility of mediation.

(26) In accordance with point 34 of the Interinstitutional agreement on better law-making,[6] Member States are encouraged to draw up, for themselves and in the interests of the Community, their own tables illustrating, as far as possible, the correlation between this Directive and the transposition measures, and to make them public.

(27) This Directive seeks to promote the fundamental rights, and takes into account the principles, recognised in particular by the Charter of Fundamental Rights of the European Union.

(28) Since the objective of this Directive cannot be sufficiently achieved by the Member States and can therefore, by reason of the scale or effects of the action, be better achieved at Community level, the Community may adopt measures in accordance with the principle of subsidiarity as set out in Article 5 of the Treaty. In accordance with the principle of proportionality, as set out in that Article, this Directive does not go beyond what is necessary in order to achieve that objective.

(29) In accordance with Article 3 of the Protocol on the position of the United Kingdom and Ireland, annexed to the Treaty on European Union and to the Treaty establishing the European Community, the United Kingdom and Ireland have given notice of their wish to take part in the adoption and application of this Directive.

(30) In accordance with Articles 1 and 2 of the Protocol on the position of Denmark, annexed to the Treaty on European Union and to the Treaty establishing the European Community, Denmark does not take part in the adoption of this Directive and is not bound by it or subject to its application,

HAVE ADOPTED THIS DIRECTIVE:

Article 1

Objective and scope

1. The objective of this Directive is to facilitate access to alternative dispute resolution and to promote the amicable settlement of disputes

by encouraging the use of mediation and by ensuring a balanced relationship between mediation and judicial proceedings.

2. This Directive shall apply, in cross-border disputes, to civil and commercial matters except as regards rights and obligations which are not at the parties' disposal under the relevant applicable law. It shall not extend, in particular, to revenue, customs or administrative matters or to the liability of the State for acts and omissions in the exercise of State authority (*acta iure imperii*).
3. In this Directive, the term 'Member State' shall mean Member States with the exception of Denmark.

Article 2

Cross-border disputes

1. For the purposes of this Directive a cross-border dispute shall be one in which at least one of the parties is domiciled or habitually resident in a Member State other than that of any other party on the date on which:
   (a) the parties agree to use mediation after the dispute has arisen;
   (b) mediation is ordered by a court;
   (c) an obligation to use mediation arises under national law; or
   (d) for the purposes of Article 5 an invitation is made to the parties.
2. Notwithstanding paragraph 1, for the purposes of Articles 7 and 8 a cross-border dispute shall also be one in which judicial proceedings or arbitration following mediation between the parties are initiated in a Member State other than that in which the parties were domiciled or habitually resident on the date referred to in paragraph 1(a), (b) or (c).
3. For the purposes of paragraphs 1 and 2, domicile shall be determined in accordance with Articles 59 and 60 of Regulation (EC) No 44/2001.

Article 3

Definitions

For the purposes of this Directive the following definitions shall apply:

(a) 'Mediation' means a structured process, however named or referred to, whereby two or more parties to a dispute attempt by themselves, on a voluntary basis, to reach an agreement on the settlement of their dispute with the assistance of a mediator. This process may be initiated by the parties or suggested or ordered by a court or prescribed by the law of a Member State.

It includes mediation conducted by a judge who is not responsible for any judicial proceedings concerning the dispute in question. It excludes attempts made by the court or the judge seised to settle a dispute in the course of judicial proceedings concerning the dispute in question.

(b) 'Mediator' means any third person who is asked to conduct a mediation in an effective, impartial and competent way, regardless of the denomination or profession of that third person in the Member State concerned and of the way in which the third person has been appointed or requested to conduct the mediation.

Article 4

Ensuring the quality of mediation

1. Member States shall encourage, by any means which they consider appropriate, the development of, and adherence to, voluntary codes of conduct by mediators and organisations providing mediation services, as well as other effective quality control mechanisms concerning the provision of mediation services.
2. Member States shall encourage the initial and further training of mediators in order to ensure that the mediation is conducted in an effective, impartial and competent way in relation to the parties.

Article 5

Recourse to mediation

1. A court before which an action is brought may, when appropriate and having regard to all the circumstances of the case, invite the parties to use mediation in order to settle the dispute. The court may also invite the parties to attend an information session on the use of mediation if such sessions are held and are easily available.
2. This Directive is without prejudice to national legislation making the use of mediation compulsory or subject to incentives or sanctions, whether before or after judicial proceedings have started, provided that such legislation does not prevent the parties from exercising their right of access to the judicial system.

Article 6

Enforceability of agreements resulting from mediation

1. Member States shall ensure that it is possible for the parties, or for one of them with the explicit consent of the others, to request that the content of a written agreement resulting from mediation be made enforceable. The content of such an agreement shall be made enforceable unless, in the case in question, either the content of that agreement is contrary to the law of the Member State where the request is made or the law of that Member State does not provide for its enforceability.
2. The content of the agreement may be made enforceable by a court or other competent authority in a judgment or decision or in an authentic instrument in accordance with the law of the Member State where the request is made.
3. Member States shall inform the Commission of the courts or other authorities competent to receive requests in accordance with paragraphs 1 and 2.
4. Nothing in this Article shall affect the rules applicable to the recognition and enforcement in another Member State of an agreement made enforceable in accordance with paragraph 1.

Article 7

Confidentiality of mediation

1. Given that mediation is intended to take place in a manner which respects confidentiality, Member States shall ensure that, unless the parties agree otherwise, neither mediators nor those involved in the administration of the mediation process shall be compelled to give evidence in civil and commercial judicial proceedings or arbitration regarding information arising out of or in connection with a mediation process, except:
   (a) where this is necessary for overriding considerations of public policy of the Member State concerned, in particular when required to ensure the protection of the best interests of children or to prevent harm to the physical or psychological integrity of a person; or
   (b) where disclosure of the content of the agreement resulting from mediation is necessary in order to implement or enforce that agreement.

2. Nothing in paragraph 1 shall preclude Member States from enacting stricter measures to protect the confidentiality of mediation.

Article 8

Effect of mediation on limitation and prescription periods

1. Member States shall ensure that parties who choose mediation in an attempt to settle a dispute are not subsequently prevented from initiating judicial proceedings or arbitration in relation to that dispute by the expiry of limitation or prescription periods during the mediation process.
2. Paragraph 1 shall be without prejudice to provisions on limitation or prescription periods in international agreements to which Member States are party.

Article 9

Information for the general public

Member States shall encourage, by any means which they consider appropriate, the availability to the general public, in particular on the Internet, of information on how to contact mediators and organisations providing mediation services.

Article 10

Information on competent courts and authorities

The Commission shall make publicly available, by any appropriate means, information on the competent courts or authorities communicated by the Member States pursuant to Article 6(3).

Article 11

Review

Not later than 21 May 2016, the Commission shall submit to the European Parliament, the Council and the European Economic and Social

Committee a report on the application of this Directive. The report shall consider the development of mediation throughout the European Union and the impact of this Directive in the Member States. If necessary, the report shall be accompanied by proposals to adapt this Directive.

Article 12

Transposition

1. Member States shall bring into force the laws, regulations, and administrative provisions necessary to comply with this Directive before 21 May 2011, with the exception of Article 10, for which the date of compliance shall be 21 November 2010 at the latest. They shall forthwith inform the Commission thereof. When they are adopted by Member States, these measures shall contain a reference to this Directive or shall be accompanied by such reference on the occasion of their official publication. The methods of making such reference shall be laid down by Member States.
2. Member States shall communicate to the Commission the text of the main provisions of national law which they adopt in the field covered by this Directive.

Article 13

Entry into force

This Directive shall enter into force on the 20th day following its publication in the *Official Journal of the European Union.*

Article 14

Addressees

This Directive is addressed to the Member States.

Done at Strasbourg, 21 May 2008.

Notes

1. OJ C 286, 17.11.2005, p. 1.
2. Opinion of the European Parliament of 29 March 2007 (OJ C 27 E, 31.1.2008, p. 129). Council Common Position of 28 February 2008 (not yet published in the Official Journal) and Position of the European Parliament of 23 April 2008 (not yet published in the Official Journal).
3. Commission Recommendation 2001/310/EC of 4 April 2001 on the principles for out-of-court bodies involved in the consensual resolution of consumer disputes (OJ L 109, 19.4.2001, p. 56).
4. OJ L 12, 16.1.2001, p. 1. Regulation as last amended by Regulation (EC) No 1791/2006 (OJ L 363, 20.12.2006, p. 1).
5. OJ L 338, 23.12.2003, p. 1. Regulation as amended by Regulation (EC) No 2116/2004 (OJ L 367, 14.12.2004, p. 1).
6. OJ C 321, 31.12.2003, p. 1.

Appendix C
The UNCITRAL Model Law on International Commercial Arbitration 1985

UNITED NATIONS

UNCITRAL Model Law on International Commercial Arbitration 1985

With amendments as adopted in 2006

UNCITRAL UNITED NATIONS COMMISSION ON INTERNATIONAL TRADE LAW

UNITED NATIONS

Vienna, 2008

UNCITRAL Model Law on International Commercial Arbitration (United Nations documents A/40/17, annex I and A/61/17, annex I)

(As adopted by the United Nations Commission on International Trade Law on 21 June 1985, and as amended by the United Nations Commission on International Trade Law on 7 July 2006)

Resolutions adopted by the General Assembly

40/72. Model Law on International Commercial Arbitration of the United Nations Commission on International Trade Law

The General Assembly,

Recognizing the value of arbitration as a method of settling disputes arising in international commercial relations,

Convinced that the establishment of a model law on arbitration that is acceptable to States with different legal, social and economic systems contributes to the development of harmonious international economic relations,

Noting that the Model Law on International Commercial Arbitration[1] was adopted by the United Nations Commission on International Trade Law at its eighteenth session, after due deliberation and extensive consultation with arbitral institutions and individual experts on international commercial arbitration,

Convinced that the Model Law, together with the Convention on the Recognition and Enforcement of Foreign Arbitral Awards[2] and the Arbitration Rules of the United Nations Commission on International Trade Law[3] recommended by the General Assembly in its resolution 31/98 of 15 December 1976, significantly contributes to the establishment of a unified legal framework for the fair and efficient settlement of disputes arising in international commercial relations,

1. *Requests* the Secretary-General to transmit the text of the Model Law on International Commercial Arbitration of the United Nations Commission on International Trade Law, together with the *travaux préparatoires* from the eighteenth session of the Commission, to Governments and to arbitral institutions and other interested bodies, such as chambers of commerce;
2. *Recommends* that all States give due consideration to the Model Law on International Commercial Arbitration, in view of the desirability of uniformity of the law of arbitral procedures and the specific needs of international commercial arbitration practice.

112th plenary meeting

11 December 1985

[*on the report of the Sixth Committee (A/61/453)*]

61/33. Revised articles of the Model Law on International Commercial Arbitration of the United Nations Commission on International Trade Law, and the recommendation regarding the interpretation of article II, paragraph 2, and article VII, paragraph 1, of the Convention on the Recognition and Enforcement of Foreign Arbitral Awards, done at New York, 10 June 1958

The General Assembly,

Recognizing the value of arbitration as a method of settling disputes arising in the context of international commercial relations,

Recalling its resolution 40/72 of 11 December 1985 regarding the Model Law on International Commercial Arbitration,[4]

Recognizing the need for provisions in the Model Law to conform to current practices in international trade and modern means of contracting with regard to the form of the arbitration agreement and the granting of interim measures,

Believing that revised articles of the Model Law on the form of the arbitration agreement and interim measures reflecting those current practices will significantly enhance the operation of the Model Law,

Noting that the preparation of the revised articles of the Model Law on the form of the arbitration agreement and interim measures was the subject of due deliberation and extensive consultations with Governments and interested circles and would contribute significantly to the establishment of a harmonized legal framework for a fair and efficient settlement of international commercial disputes,

Believing that, in connection with the modernization of articles of the Model Law, the promotion of a uniform interpretation and application of the Convention on the Recognition and Enforcement of Foreign Arbitral Awards, done at New York, 10 June 1958,[5] is particularly timely,

1. *Expresses its appreciation* to the United Nations Commission on International Trade Law for formulating and adopting the revised articles of its Model Law on International Commercial Arbitration on the form of the arbitration agreement and interim measures, the text of which is contained in annex I to the report of the United Nations Commission on International Trade Law on the work of its thirty-ninth session,[6] and recommends that all States give favourable consideration to the enactment of the revised articles of the Model Law, or the revised Model Law on International Commercial Arbitration of the United Nations Commission International Trade Law, when they enact or revise their laws, in view of the desirability of uniformity of the law of arbitral procedures and the specific needs of international commercial arbitration practice;
2. *Also expresses its appreciation* to the United Nations Commission on International Trade Law for formulating and adopting the recommendation regarding the interpretation of article II, paragraph 2,

and article VII, paragraph 1, of the Convention on the Recognition and Enforcement of Foreign Arbitral Awards, done at New York, 10 June 1958, the text of which is contained in annex II to the report of the United Nations Commission on International Trade Law on the work of its thirty-ninth session;

3. *Requests* the Secretary-General to make all efforts to ensure that the revised articles of the Model Law and the recommendation become generally known and available.

64th plenary meeting
4 December 2006

CHAPTER I. GENERAL PROVISIONS

Article 1. Scope of application[7]

(1) This Law applies to international commercial[8] arbitration, subject to any agreement in force between this State and any other State or States.

(2) The provisions of this Law, except articles 8, 9, 17 H, 17 I, 17 J, 35 and 36, apply only if the place of arbitration is in the territory of this State.

(Article 1(2) has been amended by the Commission at its thirty-ninth session, in 2006)

(3) An arbitration is international if:

(a) the parties to an arbitration agreement have, at the time of the conclusion of that agreement, their places of business in different States; or

(b) one of the following places is situated outside the State in which the parties have their places of business:

(i) the place of arbitration if determined in, or pursuant to, the arbitration agreement;

(ii) any place where a substantial part of the obligations of the commercial relationship is to be performed or the place with which the subject-matter of the dispute is most closely connected; or

(c) the parties have expressly agreed that the subject matter of the arbitration agreement relates to more than one country.

(4) For the purposes of paragraph (3) of this article:

(*a*) if a party has more than one place of business, the place of business is that which has the closest relationship to the arbitration agreement;

(*b*) if a party does not have a place of business, reference is to be made to his habitual residence.

(5) This Law shall not affect any other law of this State by virtue of which certain disputes may not be submitted to arbitration or may be submitted to arbitration only according to provisions other than those of this Law.

Article 2. Definitions and rules of interpretation

For the purposes of this Law:

(*a*) 'arbitration' means any arbitration whether or not administered by a permanent arbitral institution;

(*b*) 'arbitral tribunal' means a sole arbitrator or a panel of arbitrators;

(*c*) 'court' means a body or organ of the judicial system of a State;

(*d*) where a provision of this Law, except article 28, leaves the parties free to determine a certain issue, such freedom includes the right of the parties to authorize a third party, including an institution, to make that determination;

(*e*) where a provision of this Law refers to the fact that the parties have agreed or that they may agree or in any other way refers to an agreement of the parties, such agreement includes any arbitration rules referred to in that agreement;

(*f*) where a provision of this Law, other than in articles 25(*a*) and 32(2)(*a*), refers to a claim, it also applies to a counter-claim, and where it refers to a defence, it also applies to a defence to such counter-claim.

Article 2 A. International origin and general principles

(As adopted by the Commission at its thirty-ninth session, in 2006)

(1) In the interpretation of this Law, regard is to be had to its international origin and to the need to promote uniformity in its application and the observance of good faith.

(2) Questions concerning matters governed by this Law which are not expressly settled in it are to be settled in conformity with the general principles on which this Law is based.

Article 3. Receipt of written communications

(1) Unless otherwise agreed by the parties:

(a) any written communication is deemed to have been received if it is delivered to the addressee personally or if it is delivered at his place of business, habitual residence or mailing address; if none of these can be found after making a reasonable inquiry, a written communication is deemed to have been received if it is sent to the addressee's last-known place of business, habitual residence or mailing address by registered letter or any other means which provides a record of the attempt to deliver it;

(b) the communication is deemed to have been received on the day it is so delivered.

(2) The provisions of this article do not apply to communications in court proceedings.

Article 4. Waiver of right to object

A party who knows that any provision of this Law from which the parties may derogate or any requirement under the arbitration agreement has not been complied with and yet proceeds with the arbitration without stating his objection to such non-compliance without undue delay or, if a time-limit is provided therefore, within such period of time, shall be deemed to have waived his right to object.

Article 5. Extent of court intervention

In matters governed by this Law, no court shall intervene except where so provided in this Law.

Article 6. Court or other authority for certain functions of arbitration assistance and supervision

The functions referred to in articles 11(3), 11(4), 13(3), 14, 16(3) and 34(2) shall be performed by... [Each State enacting this model law specifies the court, courts or, where referred to therein, other authority competent to perform these functions.]

CHAPTER II. ARBITRATION AGREEMENT

Option I

Article 7. Definition and form of arbitration agreement

(As adopted by the Commission at its thirty-ninth session, in 2006)

(1) 'Arbitration agreement' is an agreement by the parties to submit to arbitration all or certain disputes which have arisen or which may arise between them in respect of a defined legal relationship, whether contractual or not. An arbitration agreement may be in the form of an arbitration clause in a contract or in the form of a separate agreement.

(2) The arbitration agreement shall be in writing.

(3) An arbitration agreement is in writing if its content is recorded in any form, whether or not the arbitration agreement or contract has been concluded orally, by conduct, or by other means.

(4) The requirement that an arbitration agreement be in writing is met by an electronic communication if the information contained therein is accessible so as to be useable for subsequent reference; 'electronic communication' means any communication that the parties make by means of data messages; 'data message' means information generated, sent, received or stored by electronic, magnetic, optical or similar means, including, but not limited to, electronic data interchange (EDI), electronic mail, telegram, telex or telecopy.

(5) Furthermore, an arbitration agreement is in writing if it is contained in an exchange of statements of claim and defence in which the existence of an agreement is alleged by one party and not denied by the other.

(6) The reference in a contract to any document containing an arbitration clause constitutes an arbitration agreement in writing, provided that the reference is such as to make that clause part of the contract.

Option II

Article 7. Definition of arbitration agreement

(As adopted by the Commission at its thirty-ninth session, in 2006)

'Arbitration agreement' is an agreement by the parties to submit to arbitration all or certain disputes which have arisen or which may arise between them in respect of a defined legal relationship, whether contractual or not.

Article 8. Arbitration agreement and substantive claim before court

(1) A court before which an action is brought in a matter which is the subject of an arbitration agreement shall, if a party so requests not later than when submitting his first statement on the substance of the dispute, refer the parties to arbitration unless it finds that the agreement is null and void, inoperative or incapable of being performed.

(2) Where an action referred to in paragraph (1) of this article has been brought, arbitral proceedings may nevertheless be commenced or continued, and an award may be made, while the issue is pending before the court.

Article 9. Arbitration agreement and interim measures by court

It is not incompatible with an arbitration agreement for a party to request, before or during arbitral proceedings, from a court an interim measure of protection and for a court to grant such measure.

CHAPTER III. COMPOSITION OF ARBITRAL TRIBUNAL

Article 10. Number of arbitrators

(1) The parties are free to determine the number of arbitrators.

(2) Failing such determination, the number of arbitrators shall be three.

Article 11. Appointment of arbitrators

(1) No person shall be precluded by reason of his nationality from acting as an arbitrator, unless otherwise agreed by the parties.

(2) The parties are free to agree on a procedure of appointing the arbitrator or arbitrators, subject to the provisions of paragraphs (4) and (5) of this article.

(3) Failing such agreement,

(a) in an arbitration with three arbitrators, each party shall appoint one arbitrator, and the two arbitrators thus appointed shall appoint the third arbitrator; if a party fails to appoint the arbitrator within thirty days of receipt of a request to do so from the other party, or if the two arbitrators fail to agree on the third arbitrator within thirty days of their appointment, the appointment shall be made, upon request of a party, by the court or other authority specified in article 6;

(b) in an arbitration with a sole arbitrator, if the parties are unable to agree on the arbitrator, he shall be appointed, upon request of a party, by the court or other authority specified in article 6.

(4) Where, under an appointment procedure agreed upon by the parties,

(a) a party fails to act as required under such procedure, or

(b) the parties, or two arbitrators, are unable to reach an agreement expected of them under such procedure, or

(c) a third party, including an institution, fails to perform any function entrusted to it under such procedure, any party may request the court or other authority specified in article 6 to take the necessary measure, unless the agreement on the appointment procedure provides other means for securing the appointment.

(5) A decision on a matter entrusted by paragraph (3) or (4) of this article to the court or other authority specified in article 6 shall be subject to no appeal. The court or other authority, in appointing an arbitrator, shall have due regard to any qualifications required of the arbitrator by the agreement of the parties and to such considerations as are likely to secure the appointment of an independent and impartial arbitrator and, in the case of a sole or third arbitrator, shall take into account as well the advisability of appointing an arbitrator of a nationality other than those of the parties.

Article 12. Grounds for challenge

(1) When a person is approached in connection with his possible appointment as an arbitrator, he shall disclose any circumstances likely to give rise to justifiable doubts as to his impartiality or independence. An arbitrator, from the time of his appointment and throughout the arbitral proceedings, shall without delay disclose any such circumstances to the parties unless they have already been informed of them by him.

(2) An arbitrator may be challenged only if circumstances exist that give rise to justifiable doubts as to his impartiality or independence, or if he does not possess qualifications agreed to by the parties. A party may challenge an arbitrator appointed by him, or in whose appointment he has participated, only for reasons of which he becomes aware after the appointment has been made.

Article 13. Challenge procedure

(1) The parties are free to agree on a procedure for challenging an arbitrator, subject to the provisions of paragraph (3) of this article.

(2) Failing such agreement, a party who intends to challenge an arbitrator shall, within fifteen days after becoming aware of the constitution of the arbitral tribunal or after becoming aware of any circumstance referred to in article 12(2), send a written statement of the reasons for the challenge to the arbitral tribunal. Unless the challenged arbitrator withdraws from his office or the other party agrees to the challenge, the arbitral tribunal shall decide on the challenge.

(3) If a challenge under any procedure agreed upon by the parties or under the procedure of paragraph (2) of this article is not successful, the challenging party may request, within thirty days after having received notice of the decision rejecting the challenge, the court or other authority specified in article 6 to decide on the challenge, which decision shall be subject to no appeal; while such a request is pending, the arbitral tribunal, including the challenged arbitrator, may continue the arbitral proceedings and make an award.

Article 14. Failure or impossibility to act

(1) If an arbitrator becomes *de jure* or *de facto* unable to perform his functions or for other reasons fails to act without undue delay, his

mandate terminates if he withdraws from his office or if the parties agree on the termination. Otherwise, if a controversy remains concerning any of these grounds, any party may request the court or other authority specified in article 6 to decide on the termination of the mandate, which decision shall be subject to no appeal.

(2) If, under this article or article 13(2), an arbitrator withdraws from his office or a party agrees to the termination of the mandate of an arbitrator, this does not imply acceptance of the validity of any ground referred to in this article or article 12(2).

Article 15. Appointment of substitute arbitrator

Where the mandate of an arbitrator terminates under article 13 or 14 or because of his withdrawal from office for any other reason or because of the revocation of his mandate by agreement of the parties or in any other case of termination of his mandate, a substitute arbitrator shall be appointed according to the rules that were applicable to the appointment of the arbitrator being replaced.

CHAPTER IV. JURISDICTION OF ARBITRAL TRIBUNAL

Article 16. Competence of arbitral tribunal to rule on its jurisdiction

(1) The arbitral tribunal may rule on its own jurisdiction, including any objections with respect to the existence or validity of the arbitration agreement. For that purpose, an arbitration clause which forms part of a contract shall be treated as an agreement independent of the other terms of the contract. A decision by the arbitral tribunal that the contract is null and void shall not entail *ipso jure* the invalidity of the arbitration clause.

(2) A plea that the arbitral tribunal does not have jurisdiction shall be raised not later than the submission of the statement of defence. A party is not precluded from raising such a plea by the fact that he has appointed, or participated in the appointment of, an arbitrator. A plea that the arbitral tribunal is exceeding the scope of its authority shall be raised as soon as the matter alleged to be beyond the scope of its authority is raised during the arbitral proceedings. The arbitral tribunal may, in either case, admit a later plea if it considers the delay justified.

(3) The arbitral tribunal may rule on a plea referred to in paragraph (2) of this article either as a preliminary question or in an award on the merits. If the arbitral tribunal rules as a preliminary question that it has jurisdiction, any party may request, within thirty days after having received notice of that ruling, the court specified in article 6 to decide the matter, which decision shall be subject to no appeal; while such a request is pending, the arbitral tribunal may continue the arbitral proceedings and make an award.

CHAPTER IV A. INTERIM MEASURES AND PRELIMINARY ORDERS

(As adopted by the Commission at its thirty-ninth session, in 2006)

Section 1. Interim measures

Article 17. Power of arbitral tribunal to order interim measures

(1) Unless otherwise agreed by the parties, the arbitral tribunal may, at the request of a party, grant interim measures.

(2) An interim measure is any temporary measure, whether in the form of an award or in another form, by which, at any time prior to the issuance of the award by which the dispute is finally decided, the arbitral tribunal orders a party to:

(a) Maintain or restore the status quo pending determination of the dispute;

(b) Take action that would prevent, or refrain from taking action that is likely to cause, current or imminent harm or prejudice to the arbitral process itself;

(c) Provide a means of preserving assets out of which a subsequent award may be satisfied; or

(d) Preserve evidence that may be relevant and material to the resolution of the dispute.

Article 17 A. Conditions for granting interim measures

(1) The party requesting an interim measure under article 17(2)*(a)*, *(b)* and *(c)* shall satisfy the arbitral tribunal that:

(a) Harm not adequately reparable by an award of damages is likely to result if the measure is not ordered, and such harm substantially outweighs the harm that is likely to result to the party against whom the measure is directed if the measure is granted; and

(b) There is a reasonable possibility that the requesting party will succeed on the merits of the claim. The determination on this possibility shall not affect the discretion of the arbitral tribunal in making any subsequent determination.

(2) With regard to a request for an interim measure under article 17(2)*(d)*, the requirements in paragraphs (1)*(a)* and *(b)* of this article shall apply only to the extent the arbitral tribunal considers appropriate.

Section 2. Preliminary orders

Article 17 B. Applications for preliminary orders and conditions for granting preliminary orders

(1) Unless otherwise agreed by the parties, a party may, without notice to any other party, make a request for an interim measure together with an application for a preliminary order directing a party not to frustrate the purpose of the interim measure requested.

(2) The arbitral tribunal may grant a preliminary order provided it considers that prior disclosure of the request for the interim measure to the party against whom it is directed risks frustrating the purpose of the measure.

(3) The conditions defined under article 17A apply to any preliminary order, provided that the harm to be assessed under article 17A(1)*(a)*, is the harm likely to result from the order being granted or not.

Article 17 C. Specific regime for preliminary orders

(1) Immediately after the arbitral tribunal has made a determination in respect of an application for a preliminary order, the arbitral tribunal shall give notice to all parties of the request for the interim measure, the application for the preliminary order, the preliminary order, if any, and all other communications, including by indicating the content of any oral communication, between any party and the arbitral tribunal in relation thereto.

(2) At the same time, the arbitral tribunal shall give an opportunity to any party against whom a preliminary order is directed to present its case at the earliest practicable time.

(3) The arbitral tribunal shall decide promptly on any objection to the preliminary order.

(4) A preliminary order shall expire after twenty days from the date on which it was issued by the arbitral tribunal. However, the arbitral tribunal may issue an interim measure adopting or modifying the preliminary order, after the party against whom the preliminary order is directed has been given notice and an opportunity to present its case.

(5) A preliminary order shall be binding on the parties but shall not be subject to enforcement by a court. Such a preliminary order does not constitute an award.

Section 3. Provisions applicable to interim measures and preliminary orders

Article 17 D. Modification, suspension, termination

The arbitral tribunal may modify, suspend or terminate an interim measure or a preliminary order it has granted, upon application of any party or, in exceptional circumstances and upon prior notice to the parties, on the arbitral tribunal's own initiative.

Article 17 E. Provision of security

(1) The arbitral tribunal may require the party requesting an interim measure to provide appropriate security in connection with the measure.

(2) The arbitral tribunal shall require the party applying for a preliminary order to provide security in connection with the order unless the arbitral tribunal considers it inappropriate or unnecessary to do so.

Article 17 F. Disclosure

(1) The arbitral tribunal may require any party promptly to disclose any material change in the circumstances on the basis of which the measure was requested or granted.

(2) The party applying for a preliminary order shall disclose to the arbitral tribunal all circumstances that are likely to be relevant to the

arbitral tribunal's determination whether to grant or maintain the order, and such obligation shall continue until the party against whom the order has been requested has had an opportunity to present its case. Thereafter, paragraph (1) of this article shall apply.

Article 17 G. Costs and damages

The party requesting an interim measure or applying for a preliminary order shall be liable for any costs and damages caused by the measure or the order to any party if the arbitral tribunal later determines that, in the circumstances, the measure or the order should not have been granted. The arbitral tribunal may award such costs and damages at any point during the proceedings.

Section 4. Recognition and enforcement of interim measures

Article 17 H. Recognition and enforcement

(1) An interim measure issued by an arbitral tribunal shall be recognized as binding and, unless otherwise provided by the arbitral tribunal, enforced upon application to the competent court, irrespective of the country in which it was issued, subject to the provisions of article 17 I.

(2) The party who is seeking or has obtained recognition or enforcement of an interim measure shall promptly inform the court of any termination, suspension or modification of that interim measure.

(3) The court of the State where recognition or enforcement is sought may, if it considers it proper, order the requesting party to provide appropriate security if the arbitral tribunal has not already made a determination with respect to security or where such a decision is necessary to protect the rights of third parties.

Article 17 I. Grounds for refusing recognition or enforcement[9]

(1) Recognition or enforcement of an interim measure may be refused only:

- *(a)* At the request of the party against whom it is invoked if the court is satisfied that:
  - (i) Such refusal is warranted on the grounds set forth in article 36(1)*(a)*(i), (ii), (iii) or (iv); or

(ii) The arbitral tribunal's decision with respect to the provision of security in connection with the interim measure issued by the arbitral tribunal has not been complied with; or

(iii) The interim measure has been terminated or suspended by the arbitral tribunal or, where so empowered, by the court of the State in which the arbitration takes place or under the law of which that interim measure was granted; or

(b) If the court finds that:

(i) The interim measure is incompatible with the powers conferred upon the court unless the court decides to reformulate the interim measure to the extent necessary to adapt it to its own powers and procedures for the purposes of enforcing that interim measure and without modifying its substance; or

(ii) Any of the grounds set forth in article 36(1)*(b)*(i) or (ii), apply to the recognition and enforcement of the interim measure.

(2) Any determination made by the court on any ground in paragraph (1) of this article shall be effective only for the purposes of the application to recognize and enforce the interim measure. The court where recognition or enforcement is sought shall not, in making that determination, undertake a review of the substance of the interim measure.

Section 5. Court-ordered interim measures

Article 17 J. Court-ordered interim measures

A court shall have the same power of issuing an interim measure in relation to arbitration proceedings, irrespective of whether their place is in the territory of this State, as it has in relation to proceedings in courts. The court shall exercise such power in accordance with its own procedures in consideration of the specific features of international arbitration.

CHAPTER V. CONDUCT OF ARBITRAL PROCEEDINGS

Article 18. Equal treatment of parties

The parties shall be treated with equality and each party shall be given a full opportunity of presenting his case.

Article 19. Determination of rules of procedure

(1) Subject to the provisions of this Law, the parties are free to agree on the procedure to be followed by the arbitral tribunal in conducting the proceedings.

(2) Failing such agreement, the arbitral tribunal may, subject to the provisions of this Law, conduct the arbitration in such manner as it considers appropriate. The power conferred upon the arbitral tribunal includes the power to determine the admissibility, relevance, materiality and weight of any evidence.

Article 20. Place of arbitration

(1) The parties are free to agree on the place of arbitration. Failing such agreement, the place of arbitration shall be determined by the arbitral tribunal having regard to the circumstances of the case, including the convenience of the parties.

(2) Notwithstanding the provisions of paragraph (1) of this article, the arbitral tribunal may, unless otherwise agreed by the parties, meet at any place it considers appropriate for consultation among its members, for hearing witnesses, experts or the parties, or for inspection of goods, other property or documents.

Article 21. Commencement of arbitral proceedings

Unless otherwise agreed by the parties, the arbitral proceedings in respect of a particular dispute commence on the date on which a request for that dispute to be referred to arbitration is received by the respondent.

Article 22. Language

(1) The parties are free to agree on the language or languages to be used in the arbitral proceedings. Failing such agreement, the arbitral tribunal shall determine the language or languages to be used in the proceedings. This agreement or determination, unless otherwise specified therein, shall apply to any written statement by a party, any hearing and any award, decision or other communication by the arbitral tribunal.

(2) The arbitral tribunal may order that any documentary evidence shall be accompanied by a translation into the language or languages agreed upon by the parties or determined by the arbitral tribunal.

Article 23. Statements of claim and defence

(1) Within the period of time agreed by the parties or determined by the arbitral tribunal, the claimant shall state the facts supporting his claim, the points at issue and the relief or remedy sought, and the respondent shall state his defence in respect of these particulars, unless the parties have otherwise agreed as to the required elements of such statements. The parties may submit with their statements all documents they consider to be relevant or may add a reference to the documents or other evidence they will submit.

(2) Unless otherwise agreed by the parties, either party may amend or supplement his claim or defence during the course of the arbitral proceedings, unless the arbitral tribunal considers it inappropriate to allow such amendment having regard to the delay in making it.

Article 24. Hearings and written proceedings

(1) Subject to any contrary agreement by the parties, the arbitral tribunal shall decide whether to hold oral hearings for the presentation of evidence or for oral argument, or whether the proceedings shall be conducted on the basis of documents and other materials. However, unless the parties have agreed that no hearings shall be held, the arbitral tribunal shall hold such hearings at an appropriate stage of the proceedings, if so requested by a party.

(2) The parties shall be given sufficient advance notice of any hearing and of any meeting of the arbitral tribunal for the purposes of inspection of goods, other property or documents.

(3) All statements, documents or other information supplied to the arbitral tribunal by one party shall be communicated to the other party. Also any expert report or evidentiary document on which the arbitral tribunal may rely in making its decision shall be communicated to the parties.

Article 25. Default of a party

Unless otherwise agreed by the parties, if, without showing sufficient cause,

(a) the claimant fails to communicate his statement of claim in accordance with article 23(1), the arbitral tribunal shall terminate the proceedings;

(b) the respondent fails to communicate his statement of defence in accordance with article 23(1), the arbitral tribunal shall continue the proceedings without treating such failure in itself as an admission of the claimant's allegations;

(c) any party fails to appear at a hearing or to produce documentary evidence, the arbitral tribunal may continue the proceedings and make the award on the evidence before it.

Article 26. Expert appointed by arbitral tribunal

(1) Unless otherwise agreed by the parties, the arbitral tribunal

(a) may appoint one or more experts to report to it on specific issues to be determined by the arbitral tribunal;

(b) may require a party to give the expert any relevant information or to produce, or to provide access to, any relevant documents, goods or other property for his inspection.

(2) Unless otherwise agreed by the parties, if a party so requests or if the arbitral tribunal considers it necessary, the expert shall, after delivery of his written or oral report, participate in a hearing where the parties have the opportunity to put questions to him and to present expert witnesses in order to testify on the points at issue.

Article 27. Court assistance in taking evidence

The arbitral tribunal or a party with the approval of the arbitral tribunal may request from a competent court of this State assistance in taking evidence. The court may execute the request within its competence and according to its rules on taking evidence.

CHAPTER VI. MAKING OF AWARD AND TERMINATION OF PROCEEDINGS

Article 28. Rules applicable to substance of dispute

(1) The arbitral tribunal shall decide the dispute in accordance with such rules of law as are chosen by the parties as applicable to the substance of the dispute. Any designation of the law or legal system of a given State shall be construed, unless otherwise expressed, as

directly referring to the substantive law of that State and not to its conflict of laws rules.

(2) Failing any designation by the parties, the arbitral tribunal shall apply the law determined by the conflict of laws rules which it considers applicable.

(3) The arbitral tribunal shall decide *ex aequo et bono* or as *amiable compositeur* only if the parties have expressly authorized it to do so.

(4) In all cases, the arbitral tribunal shall decide in accordance with the terms of the contract and shall take into account the usages of the trade applicable to the transaction.

Article 29. Decision-making by panel of arbitrators

In arbitral proceedings with more than one arbitrator, any decision of the arbitral tribunal shall be made, unless otherwise agreed by the parties, by a majority of all its members. However, questions of procedure may be decided by a presiding arbitrator, if so authorized by the parties or all members of the arbitral tribunal.

Article 30. Settlement

(1) If, during arbitral proceedings, the parties settle the dispute, the arbitral tribunal shall terminate the proceedings and, if requested by the parties and not objected to by the arbitral tribunal, record the settlement in the form of an arbitral award on agreed terms.

(2) An award on agreed terms shall be made in accordance with the provisions of article 31 and shall state that it is an award. Such an award has the same status and effect as any other award on the merits of the case.

Article 31. Form and contents of award

(1) The award shall be made in writing and shall be signed by the arbitrator or arbitrators. In arbitral proceedings with more than one arbitrator, the signatures of the majority of all members of the arbitral tribunal shall suffice, provided that the reason for any omitted signature is stated.

(2) The award shall state the reasons upon which it is based, unless the parties have agreed that no reasons are to be given or the award is an award on agreed terms under article 30.

(3) The award shall state its date and the place of arbitration as determined in accordance with article 20(1). The award shall be deemed to have been made at that place.

(4) After the award is made, a copy signed by the arbitrators in accordance with paragraph (1) of this article shall be delivered to each party.

Article 32. Termination of proceedings

(1) The arbitral proceedings are terminated by the final award or by an order of the arbitral tribunal in accordance with paragraph (2) of this article.

(2) The arbitral tribunal shall issue an order for the termination of the arbitral proceedings when:

(a) the claimant withdraws his claim, unless the respondent objects thereto and the arbitral tribunal recognizes a legitimate interest on his part in obtaining a final settlement of the dispute;

(b) the parties agree on the termination of the proceedings;

(c) the arbitral tribunal finds that the continuation of the proceedings has for any other reason become unnecessary or impossible.

(3) The mandate of the arbitral tribunal terminates with the termination of the arbitral proceedings, subject to the provisions of articles 33 and 34(4).

Article 33. Correction and interpretation of award; additional award

(1) Within thirty days of receipt of the award, unless another period of time has been agreed upon by the parties:

(a) a party, with notice to the other party, may request the arbitral tribunal to correct in the award any errors in computation, any clerical or typographical errors or any errors of similar nature;

(b) if so agreed by the parties, a party, with notice to the other party, may request the arbitral tribunal to give an interpretation of a specific point or part of the award.

If the arbitral tribunal considers the request to be justified, it shall make the correction or give the interpretation within thirty days of receipt of the request. The interpretation shall form part of the award.

(2) The arbitral tribunal may correct any error of the type referred to in paragraph (1)*(a)* of this article on its own initiative within thirty days of the date of the award.

(3) Unless otherwise agreed by the parties, a party, with notice to the other party, may request, within thirty days of receipt of the award, the arbitral tribunal to make an additional award as to claims presented in the arbitral proceedings but omitted from the award. If the arbitral tribunal considers the request to be justified, it shall make the additional award within sixty days.

(4) The arbitral tribunal may extend, if necessary, the period of time within which it shall make a correction, interpretation or an additional award under paragraph (1) or (3) of this article.

(5) The provisions of article 31 shall apply to a correction or interpretation of the award or to an additional award.

CHAPTER VII. RECOURSE AGAINST AWARD

Article 34. Application for setting aside as exclusive recourse against arbitral award

(1) Recourse to a court against an arbitral award may be made only by an application for setting aside in accordance with paragraphs (2) and (3) of this article.

(2) An arbitral award may be set aside by the court specified in article 6 only if:

(a) the party making the application furnishes proof that:

(i) a party to the arbitration agreement referred to in article 7 was under some incapacity; or the said agreement is not valid under the law to which the parties have subjected it or, failing any indication thereon, under the law of this State; or

(ii) the party making the application was not given proper notice of the appointment of an arbitrator or of the arbitral proceedings or was otherwise unable to present his case; or

(iii) the award deals with a dispute not contemplated by or not falling within the terms of the submission to arbitration, or contains decisions on matters beyond the scope of the submission to arbitration, provided that, if the decisions on matters submitted to arbitration can be separated from those not so submitted, only that part of the award which contains decisions on matters not submitted to arbitration may be set aside; or

(iv) the composition of the arbitral tribunal or the arbitral procedure was not in accordance with the agreement of the parties, unless such agreement was in conflict with a provision of this Law from which the parties cannot derogate, or, failing such agreement, was not in accordance with this Law; or

(b) the court finds that:

(i) the subject-matter of the dispute is not capable of settlement by arbitration under the law of this State; or

(ii) the award is in conflict with the public policy of this State.

(3) An application for setting aside may not be made after three months have elapsed from the date on which the party making that application had received the award or, if a request had been made under article 33, from the date on which that request had been disposed of by the arbitral tribunal.

(4) The court, when asked to set aside an award, may, where appropriate and so requested by a party, suspend the setting aside proceedings for a period of time determined by it in order to give the arbitral tribunal an opportunity to resume the arbitral proceedings or to take such other action as in the arbitral tribunal's opinion will eliminate the grounds for setting aside.

CHAPTER VIII. RECOGNITION AND ENFORCEMENT OF AWARDS

Article 35. Recognition and enforcement

(1) An arbitral award, irrespective of the country in which it was made, shall be recognized as binding and, upon application in writing to the competent court, shall be enforced subject to the provisions of this article and of article 36.

(2) The party relying on an award or applying for its enforcement shall supply the original award or a copy thereof. If the award is not made in an official language of this State, the court may request the party to supply a translation thereof into such language.[10]

(Article 35(2) has been amended by the Commission at its thirty-ninth session, in 2006)

Article 36. Grounds for refusing recognition or enforcement

(1) Recognition or enforcement of an arbitral award, irrespective of the country in which it was made, may be refused only:

(a) at the request of the party against whom it is invoked, if that party furnishes to the competent court where recognition or enforcement is sought proof that:

(i) a party to the arbitration agreement referred to in article 7 was under some incapacity; or the said agreement is not valid under the law to which the parties have subjected it or, failing any indication thereon, under the law of the country where the award was made; or

(ii) the party against whom the award is invoked was not given proper notice of the appointment of an arbitrator or of the arbitral proceedings or was otherwise unable to present his case; or

(iii) the award deals with a dispute not contemplated by or not falling within the terms of the submission to arbitration, or it contains decisions on matters beyond the scope of the submission to arbitration, provided that, if the decisions on matters submitted to arbitration can be separated from those not so submitted, that part of the award which contains decisions on matters submitted to arbitration may be recognized and enforced; or

(iv) the composition of the arbitral tribunal or the arbitral procedure was not in accordance with the agreement of the parties or, failing such agreement, was not in accordance with the law of the country where the arbitration took place; or

(v) the award has not yet become binding on the parties or has been set aside or suspended by a court of the country in which, or under the law of which, that award was made; or

(b) if the court finds that:

(i) the subject-matter of the dispute is not capable of settlement by arbitration under the law of this State; or

(ii) the recognition or enforcement of the award would be contrary to the public policy of this State.

(2) If an application for setting aside or suspension of an award has been made to a court referred to in paragraph (1)(*a*)(v) of this article, the court where recognition or enforcement is sought may, if it considers it proper, adjourn its decision and may also, on the application of the party claiming recognition or enforcement of the award, order the other party to provide appropriate security.

Notes

1. UN, Official Records of the General Assembly, 40th Session, Supplement No. 17 (A/40/17), annex I.
2. UN, *Treaty Series*, vol. 330, no. 4739, p. 38.
3. UN publication, Sales No. E.77.V.6.
4. UN, Official Records of the General Assembly, 40th Session, Supplement No. 17 (A/40/17), annex I.
5. UN, *Treaty Series*, vol. 330, No. 4739.
6. UN, Official Records of the General Assembly, 61st Session, Supplement No. 17 (A/61/17).
7. Article headings are for reference purposes only and are not to be used for purposes of interpretation.
8. The term 'commercial' should be given a wide interpretation so as to cover matters arising from all relationships of a commercial nature, whether contractual or not. Relationships of a commercial nature include, but are not limited to, the following transactions: any trade transaction for the supply or exchange of goods or services; distribution agreement; commercial representation or agency; factoring; leasing; construction of works; consulting; engineering; licensing; investment; financing; banking; insurance; exploitation agreement or concession; joint venture and other forms of industrial or business cooperation; carriage of goods or passengers by air, sea, rail or road.
9. The conditions set forth in article 17 I are intended to limit the number of circumstances in which the court may refuse to enforce an interim measure. It would not be contrary to the level of harmonisation sought to be achieved by these model provisions if a state were to adopt fewer circumstances in which enforcement may be refused.
10. The conditions set forth in this paragraph are intended to set maximum standards. Thus it would not be contrary to the harmonisation to be achieved by the model law if a state retained even less onerous conditions.

Bibliography

Books and journals

AAA (American Arbitration Association) (2006), 'AAA and Cybersettle Sign Unique Partnership Agreement', Industry News, 2 October, available at http://www.adr.org/sp.asp?id=29511 (assessed 1 June 2008).

ABA (American Bar Association) (2002a), 'Report on Mediator Credentialing and Quality Assurance', discussion draft, by ABA Section of Dispute Resolution Task Force on Credentialing, available at http://www.abanet.org/dispute/taskforce_report_2003.pdf (accessed 29 May 2008).

ABA (American Bar Association) (2002b), ABA Task Force on E-Commerce and ADR, 'Addressing Disputes in Electronic Commerce, Final Report and Recommendation', http://www.abanet.org/dispute/documents/FinalReport102802.pdf (accessed 1 June 2008).

ABA (American Bar Association) with the Shidler Center for Law, Commerce and Technology, University of Washington School of Law (2002), 'Addressing Disputes in Electronic Commerce: Final Report and Recommendations of the American Bar Association's Task Force on Electronic Commerce and Alternative Dispute Resolution', available at http://www.abanet.org/dispute/documents/FinalReport102802.pdf (accessed 28 August 2007).

ACR (Association for Conflict Resolution) (2004), ACR Task Force on Mediator Certification, 'Report and Recommendation to the Board of Directors', 31 March, available at http://www.acrnet.org/pdfs/certificationreport2004.pdf (accessed 29 May 2008).

ALA (American Library Association) (2006), 'UCITA and Related Legislation In Your State', last updated in May 2006, available at http://www.ala.org/ala/washoff/woissues/copyrightb/ucita/states.cfm (accessed 7 September 2007).

Alvaro, J.A.G. (2003), 'Online Dispute Resolution – Unchartered Territory', *Vindobona Journal of International Commercial Law and Arbitration*, vol. 7, no. 2, pp. 187–98.

Astrup, J. (2003), 'Clearing Up E-Contracting Issues', *Legal Times*, 21 July, available at http://www.uscib.org/index.asp?documentID=2696 (accessed 9 March 2005).

Ba, S. and Pavlou, P.A. (2002), 'Evidence of the Effect of Trust Building Technology in Electronic Markets: Price Premiums and Buyer Behaviour', *MIS Quarterly*, vol. 26, no. 3, pp. 243–68.

Bainbridge, D.I. (2008), *Introduction to Information Technology Law*, 6th ed. (Harlow: Pearson Longman).

Bogle, P. and Mitchell, E. (2000), 'E-Commerce Legislation in the EU', *E-Risk Management Briefing*, December.

Bonnet, V., Boudaoud, K., Gagnebin, M., Harms, J. and Schultz, T. (2004), 'Online Dispute Resolution Systems as Web Services', *ICFAI Journal of Alternative Dispute Resolution*, vol. 3, July.

Boss, A.H. (1998), 'Electronic Commerce and the Symbiotic Relationship Between International and Domestic Law Reform', *Tulane Law Review*, vol. 72, no. 6, pp. 1931–94.

Calliess, G.P. (2006), 'Online Dispute Resolution: Consumer Redress in a Global Market Place', *German Law Journal*, vol. 7, no. 8, pp. 647–60.

CCID Consulting (2007a), '2006–2007 Annual Report on China's E-Commerce Market', 30 March 2007, available at http://chinamarket.ccidnet.com/pub/enreport/show_18116.html (accessed 22 April 2007).

CCID Consulting (2007b), '2006–2007 Annual Report on the Development of Global E-Commerce Industry', available at http://chinamarket.ccidnet.com/pub/enreport/show_17192.html (accessed 22 April 2007).

China Daily (2006), 'Survey: Lack of Trust Stifles Online Trade', 5 September, available at http://www.china.org.cn/english/2006/Sep/180141.htm (accessed 22 April 2007).

Chow, D.C.K. and Schoenbaum, T.J. (2005), *International Business Transactions: Problems, Cases and Materials* (New York: Aspen Publishers).

Clark, E. and Author, H. (2002), 'Online Dispute Resolution: Present Realities and Future Prospects', available at http://www.leadr.com.au/HOYLE.PDF (accessed 21 May 2008).

Clinton, W.J. and Gore, A. (1997), 'A Framework for Global Electronic Commerce', available at http://www.w3.org/TR/NOTE-framework-970706.html#principles (accessed 19 November 2004).

CMIC (China Market Intelligence Center) (2007a), 'B2B E-Commerce Trade Valued at 888 Million RMB', 25 June, available at http://

chinamarket.ccidnet.com/market/article/content/505/200706/141565.html (accessed 26 June 2007).

CMIC (China Market Intelligence Center) (2007b), 'China's E-Commerce Enters Industrialization Era in 2007', 30 August, available at http://chinamarket.ccidnet.com/market/article/content/505/200708/170595.html (accessed 30 August 2007).

CNNIC (China Internet Network Information Center) (2007a), 'CNNIC Released the 19th Statistical Survey Report on Internet Development in China', available at http://www.cnnic.net.cn/html/Dir/2007/02/05/4432.htm (accessed 27 March 2007).

CNNIC (China Internet Network Information Center) (2007b), *Statistical Survey Report on Internet Development in China*, available at http://www.cnnic.net.cn/uploadfiles/pdf/2007/2/14/200607.pdf (accessed 27 March 2007).

Commission of the European Union (1997), A European Initiative in Electronic Commerce, COM (97) 157, available at http://cordis.europa.eu/esprit/src/ecomcom0.htm (accessed 1 June 2008).

Connolly, C. and Ravindra, P. (2005), 'UN Releases New International Convention on Electronic Contracting', Galexia Consulting, 4 January, available at http://consult.galexia.com/public/research/assets/galexia_uncitral_draft_convention_v4_20050104.pdf (accessed 28 February 2005).

Copeland, C. (2000) 'Digital Signatures: Throw Away Your Pens', *Entertainment Law Review*, vol. 11, no. 2, pp. 112–13.

Dalhuisen, J.H. (2007), *Dalhuisen on Transnational and Comparative Commercial, Financial and Trade Law*, 3rd ed. (Oxford and Portland, Oregon: Hart Publishing, 2007).

Drahozal, C.R. (2006), 'New Experience of International Arbitration in the United States, Section II: Civil Law, Procedure, and Private International Law', *American Journal of Comparative Law*, vol. 54, pp. 233–55.

EC (European Commission) (2003), 'E-Commerce: EU Law Boosting Emerging Sector', IP/03/ 1580, Brussels, 21 November, available at http://europa.eu.int/rapi.../1580&format=HTML&aged=1&language=EN&guiLanguage=e (accessed 31 October 2004).

EC (European Commission) (2005), 'eEurope, an Information Society for All', available at http://europe.eu.int/comm/information_society/eeurope/objectives/area03_en.htm (accessed 20 January 2007).

EC (European Commission) (2006), 'Legal Study on Unfair Commercial Practices within B2B e-markets – Final Report', EC Study ENTR/04/ 69.

EC (European Commission) (2008), 'Mediation in Civil and Commercial Matters', Europea press release, MEMO/08/263, Brussels, 23 April, available at http://europa.eu/rapid/pressReleasesAction.do?reference=

MEMO/08/263&type=HTML&aged=0&language=EN&guiLanguage=en (accessed 25 May 2008).

Edwards, L. and Wilson, C. (2007), 'Redress and Alternative Dispute Resolution in EU Cross-border E-Commerce Transactions', briefing note (IP/A/IMCO/IC/2006-206). IP/A/IMCO/NT/2006-31, PE 382.179, DG Internal Policies of the Union Policy Department Economic and Scientific Policy, European Parliament, available at http://www.europarl.europa.eu/comparl/imco/studies/0701_crossborder_ecom_en.pdf (accessed 3 September 2007).

EITO (European Information Technology Observatory) (n.d.), 'Electronic Commerce', policy brief, available at http://ec.europa.eu/unitedkingdom/information/policy_briefs/bb08a_en.htm (accessed 7 September 2007).

EUROSTAT (2007), 'E-Commerce via Internet: Percentage of Enterprises' Total Turnover from E-Commerce via Internet', available at http://epp.eurostat.ec.europa.eu/ (accessed 20 April 2007).

Exon, S.N. (2002), 'The Internet Meets Obi-Wan Kenobi in the Court of Next Resort', *Boston University Journal of Science and Technology Law*, vol. 8, pp. 1–36.

Faria, J.A.E. (2006), 'The United Nations Convention on the Use of Electronic Communications in International Contracts – An Introductory Note', *International and Comparative Law Quarterly*, vol. 55, pp. 689–94.

Fort, T.L. and Liu, J.H. (2002), 'Chinese Business and the Internet: The Infrastructure for Trust', *Vanderbilt Journal of Transnational Law*, vol. 35, pp. 1545–98.

Gidari, A. and Morgan, J. (2000), 'Internet Law and Policy, Update: Survey of State Electronic and Digital Signature Legislative Initiatives', available at http://www.ilpf.org/digsig/update.htm (last modified 24 September 2000).

Glatt, C. (1998), 'Comparative Issues in the Formation of Electronic Contracts (United Kingdom)', *International Journal of Law and Information Technology*, vol. 6, pp. 34–68.

Goldman, D. (2006), 'I Always Feel Like Someone is Watching Me: A Technological Solution for Online Privacy', *Hastings Communications and Entertainment Law Journal*, vol. 28, p. 353.

Goodman, J.W. (2003), 'The Pros and Cons of Online Dispute Resolution: an Assessment of Cyber-Mediation Websites', *Duke Law and Technology Review*, vol. 4, available at http://www.law.duke.edu/journals/dltr/articles/2003dltr0004.html (accessed 1 June 2008).

Hattotuwa, S. (2006), 'Transforming Landscapes: Forging New ODR Systems with a Human Face', *Conflict Resolution Quarterly*, vol. 23, no. 3, pp. 371–82.

Hayllar, M. (2000), 'The Importance and Attributes of Effective Accountability Relationships', *Asian Review of Public Administration*, vol. 12, pp. 60–80.

Hosmer, L.T. (1995), 'Trust: The Connecting Link Between Organizational Theory and Philosophical Business Ethics', *Academic Management Review*, vol. 20, pp. 379–403.

Hu, L. (2005), 'Online Arbitration in China – An Overview and Perspective', available at http://www.odr.info/ (accessed 17 August 2006).

ICC (International Chamber of Commerce) (2003), 'ICC Rules on E-Contracting Are On Their Way', Paris, 15 September, available at http:// www.iccwbo.org/home/news_archives/2003/stories/e-terms.asp (accessed 9 March 2005).

ICC (International Chamber of Commerce) (2003b) 'Resolving Disputes Online: Best Practice for Online Dispute Resolution (ODR) in B2C and C2C transactions', Tools for E-business, available at http:// www.iccwbo.org/uploadedFiles/ICC/policy/e-business/pages/ ResolvingDisputesOnline.pdf (accessed 29 May 2008).

Internet World Stats (2007), 'Internet Usage in the European Union: Internet User Statistics & Population for the 27 European Union Member States', statistics updated 30 June 2007, available at http:// www.internetworldstats.com/stats9.htm (accessed 7 September 2007).

Janićijević, D. (2005), 'Delocalization of International Commercial Arbitration', *Law and Politics*, vol. 3, no. 1, pp. 63–71, available at http://facta.junis.ni.ac.yu/lap/lap2005/lap2005-07.pdf (accessed 19 May 2008).

Katsh, E. (2007), 'Online Dispute Resolution: Some Implications for the Emergence of Law in Cyberspace', *International Review of Law Computers and Technology*, vol. 21, no. 2, pp. 97–107.

Katsh, E.M. and Rifkin, J. (2001), *Online Dispute Resolution: Resolving Conflicts in Cyberspace* (San Francisco: Jossey-Bass).

Kaufmann-Kohler, G. and Schultz, T. (2004), *Online Dispute Resolution: Challenges for Contemporary Justice* (Netherlands: Kluwer Law International).

Lewicki, R.J. and Wiethoff, C. (2000), 'Trust, Trust Development, and Trust Repair', in M. Deutsch and P. Coleman (eds), *Handbook of Conflict Resolution: Theory and Practice* (San Francisco: Jossey-Bass).

Lloyd, I.J. (2004), *Information Technology Law*, 4th ed. (Oxford: Oxford University Press).

Lodder, A.R. (2000), 'Electronic Contracts and Signatures: National Civil Law in the EU Will Change Drastically Soon', available at http://www.bileta.ac.uk/00papers/lodder.html (accessed 28 October 2004).

Lodder, A.R. (2006), 'The Third Party and Beyond: An Analysis of the Different Parties, in Particular The Fifth, Involved in Online Dispute Resolution', *Information & Communications Technology Law*, vol. 15, issue 2, pp. 143–55.

Lodder, A.R. and Zeleznikow, J. (2005), 'Developing an Online Dispute Resolution Environment: Dialogue Tools and Negotiation Support Systems in a Three-Step Model', *Harvard Negotiation Law Review*, vol. 10, pp. 287–338.

Lupton, W.E. (1999), Comment, 'The Digital Signature: Your Identity by the Numbers', *Richmond Journal of Law and Technology*, vol. 6, p. 10, available at http://www.richmond.edu/jolt/v6i2/note2.html (accessed 9 August 2004).

Mawrey, R.B. and Salmon, K.J. (1988), *Computers and the Law* (Oxford: BSP Professional Books).

Mills, K. (2004), 'Effective Formation of Contracts by Electronic Means and Dispute Resolution in the New E-conomy: Still More Questions than Answers', in N.S. Kinsella and A.F. Simpson (eds), *Online Contract Formation* (New York: Oceana Publications, Inc.).

Minow, M. (2003), 'Public and Private Partnerships: Accounting for the New Religion', *Harvard Law Review*, vol. 116, pp. 1229–70.

Moreno, C. (2001), 'Brief Overview of Selective Legal and Regulatory Issues in Electronic Commerce' at International Symposium on Government and Electronic Commerce Development, Ningbo (China), 23–24 April, available at http://unpan1.un.org/intradoc/groups/public/documents/ un/unpan001099.pdf (accessed 14 February 2005).

Motion, P. (2005), 'Article 17 ECD: Encouragement of Alternative Dispute Resolution On-line Dispute Resolution: A View From Scotland', pp. 137–69, in L. Edwards (ed.), *The New Legal Framework for E-Commerce in Europe* (Oxford: Hart Publishing, 2005).

Mutz, D.C. (2005), 'Social Trust and E-Commerce: Experimental Evidence for the Effects of Social Trust on Individuals' Economic Behavior', *Public Opinion Quarterly*, vol. 69, no. 3, pp. 393–416.

NADRAC (National Alternative Dispute Resolution Advisory Council) (2001), 'On-line ADR Background Paper', available at http://www.nadrac.gov.au/agd/WWW/disputeresolutionHome.nsf/Page/Publications_All_Publications_On_line_ADR_Background_Paper (accessed 21 May 2008).

NADRAC (National Alternative Dispute Resolution Advisory Council) (2002), 'Dispute Resolution and Information Technology: Principles of Good Practice', March, available at http://www.nadrac.gov.au/agd/WWW/rwpattach.nsf/VAP/(3A6790B96C927794AF1031D9395C5C20)~Dispute+resolution+and+information+technology.htm/$file/Dispute+resolution+and+information+technology.htm (accessed 29 May 2008).

NADRAC (National Alternative Dispute Resolution Advisory Council) (2004a), 'Who Can Refer To, or Conduct, Mediation? A Compendium of Australian Legislative Provisions Covering Referral to Mediation and Accreditation of Mediators', available at http://www.nadrac.gov.au/agd/WWW/disputeresolutionhome.nsf/Page/Legislation (accessed 29 May 2008).

NADRAC (National Alternative Dispute Resolution Advisory Council) (2004b), 'Who says you're a mediator? Towards a National System for Accrediting Mediators', prepared for a national workshop on mediation standards, facilitated by NADRAC, at the 7th National Mediation Conference in Darwin on 2 July 2004, available at http://www.nadrac.gov.au/agd/WWW/disputeresolutionHome.nsf/Page/Publications_All_Publications_Who_says_you&apos (accessed 29 May 2008).

NADRAC (National Alternative Dispute Resolution Advisory Council) (2006), 'Legislating for Alternative Dispute Resolution: A Guide for Government Policy-makers and Legal Drafters', available at http://www.nadrac.gov.au/agd/WWW/disputeresolutionHome.nsf/Page/Publications_All_Publications_Legislating_for_alternative_dispute_resolution:_A_guide_for_government_policy-makers_and_legal_drafters (accessed 26 May 2008).

Nimmer, R.T. (2001a), 'Materials on UCITA: What is It and Why is so Much Misrepresented About the Statute', 670 *PLI/PAT* 591, 619 (Westlaw).

Nimmer, R.T. (2001b), 'Understanding Electronic Contracting: UCITA, E-Signature, Federal, State, and Foreign Regulations 2001', 649 *PLI/PAT* 15, 40 (Westlaw).

OECD (Organisation for Economic Co-operation and Development) (1997a), 'Dismantling the Barriers to Global Electronic Commerce', 16 October, available at http://www.oecd.org/document/32/0,2340,en_2649_33757_1814368_1_1_1_1,00.html (accessed 21 April 2007).

OECD (Organisation for Economic Co-operation and Development) (1997b), *Electronic Commerce: Opportunities and Challenges for Government* (Paris: Organisation for Economic Co-Operation and Development).

OECD (Organisation for Economic Co-operation and Development) (2001), 'OECD Electronic Commerce Policy Brief', *OECD Observer*, July, available at http://www.oecd.org/dataoecd/5/11/2346217.pdf (accessed 15 July 2008).

OECD (Organisation for Economic Co-operation and Development) (2006), 'ICT Industry Growth Set To Increase By 6% in 2006, Says OECD', available at http://www.oecd.org/document/34/0,3343,en_2649_37441_37487522_1_1_1_37441,00.html (accessed 7 September 2007).

OECD (Organisation for Economic Co-operation and Development) (2007), 'OECD Factbook 2007 – Economic, Environmental and Social Statistics', Science and Technology, Size of the ICT Sector, available at http://miranda.sourceoecd.org/vl=25119448/cl=11/nw=1/rpsv/factbook/07-02-01.htm (accessed 20 April 2007).

Panel on Accountability and Governance in the Voluntary Sector (1999), 'Building on Strength: Improving Governance and Accountability in Canada's Voluntary Sector', cited in Rabinovich-Einy (2006), pp. 253, 261.

Pappas, C.W. (2002), 'Comparative US & EU Approaches to E-Commerce Regulation: Jurisdiction, Electronic Contracts, Electronic Signatures and Taxation (The Holland and Hart Private International Law Award)', *Denver Journal of International Law and Policy*, vol. 31, pp. 352–47.

Patrikios, A. (2006–7), 'Resolution of Cross-Border E-business Disputes by Arbitration Tribunals on the Basis of Transnational Substantive Rules of Law and E-business Usages: The Emergence of the Lex Informatica', *University of Toledo Law Review*, vol. 38, pp. 271–306.

Perritt, H.H., Jr, (1998), 'Will the Judgment-Proof Own Cyberspace?', *International Lawyer*, vol. 32, p. 1121.

Philippe, M. (2002), 'Where Is Everyone Going With Online Dispute Resolution (ODR)?', *International Business Law Journal*, vol. 2, pp. 167–210.

Poblet, M. and Casanovas, P. (2007), 'Emotions in ODR', *International Review of Law Computers and Technology*, vol. 21, no. 2, pp. 145–55.

Ponte, L.M. (2001), 'Throwing Bad Money After Bad: Can Online Dispute Resolution (ODR) Really Deliver the Goods for the Unhappy Internet Shopper?', *Tulane Journal of Technology and Intellectual Property*, vol. 3, p. 55.

Ponte, L.M. (2002), 'Boosting Consumer Confidence in E-business: Recommendations for Establishing Fair and Effective Dispute Resolution Programs for B2C Online Transactions', *Albany Law Journal of Science and Technology*, vol. 12, pp. 441–4.

Ponte, L.M. and Cavenagh, T.D. (2005), *Cyberjustice: Online Dispute Resolution (ODR) for E-Commerce* (New Jersey: Pearson Education, Inc.).

Pryles, M. ed. (2006), *Dispute Resolution in Asia*, 3rd ed. (Netherlands: Kluwer Law International).

Rabinovich-Einy, O. (2003–4), 'Balancing the Scales: the Ford-Firestone case, the Internet, and the Future Dispute Resolution Landscape', *Yale Journal of Law & Technology*, vol. 6, pp. 1–53.

Rabinovich-Einy, O. (2006), 'Technology's Impact: The Quest for a New Paradigm for Accountability in Mediation', *Harvard Negotiation Law Review*, vol. 11, pp. 253–93.

Raines, S.S. (2006), 'Mediating in Your Pyjamas: The Benefits and Challenges for ODR Practitioners', *Conflict Resolution Quarterly*, vol. 23, no. 3, pp. 359–69.

Reed, C. and Angel, J. (2007), 'Electronic Commerce', in C. Reed and J. Angel (eds), *Computer Law: The Law and Regulation of Information Technology*, 6th ed. (Oxford: Oxford University Press), pp. 197–231.

Riskin, L.L. and Westbrook, J.E. (1998), *Dispute Resolution and Lawyers*, 2nd ed. (US: West Publishing Co.).

Rosner, N. (2004), 'International Jurisdiction in European Union E-Commerce Contracts', in N.S. Kinsella and A.F. Simpson (eds), *Online Contract Formation* (New York: Oceana Publications, Inc.).

Rule, C. (2002), *Online Dispute Resolution for Business: B2B, E-Commerce, Consumer, Employment, Insurance and Other Commercial Conflicts* (San Francisco, CA: Jossey-Bass Publishing).

Schultz, T. (2004), 'Does Online Dispute Resolution Need Governmental Intervention? The Case for Architectures of Control and Trust', *North Carolina Journal of Law & Technology*, vol. 6, issue 1, p. 71.

Schulze, C. and Baumgartner, J. (2001), 'Don't Panic! Do E-Commerce: A Beginner's Guide to European Law Affecting E-Commerce, European Commission's Electronic Commerce Team, 2001', available at http://europa.eu.int/ISPO/ecommerce/books/dont_panic.pdf (accessed 10 February 2007).

Schulze, T., Kaufmann-Kohler, G., Langer, D. and Bonnet, V. (2001), 'Online Dispute Resolution: The State of the Art and the Issues', E-Com Research Project of the University of Geneva, Geneva, available at http://www.online-adr.org/reports/TheBlueBook-2001.pdf (accessed 1 June 2008).

Sekolec, J. (2007) 'General Problems of Transnational Law and its Implications for the Companies and International Trade', distinguished lecture given on 17 September 2007 to Faculty of Law, University of Deusto, Bilbao (Spain).

Spencer, D. and Brogan, M. (2006), *Mediation Law and Practice* (Melbourne: Cambridge University Press).

Stipanowich, T.J. (2001), 'Contract and Conflict Management', *Wisconsin Law Review*, pp. 831–917.

Syme, D. (2006), 'Keeping Pace: On-line Technology and ADR Services', *Conflict Resolution Quarterly*, vol. 23, no. 3, pp. 343–57.

Tao, J. (2005), *Resolving Business Disputes in China*, Asia Business Law Series (Netherlands: Kluwer Law International).

Teitz, L.E. (2005), 'The Hague Choice of Court Convention: Validating Party Autonomy and Providing an Alternative to Arbitration', *American Journal of Comparative Law*, vol. 53, pp. 543–58.

Terrett, A. and Monaghan, I. (2000), 'The Internet – An Introduction for Lawyers', in L. Edwards and C. Waelde (eds), *Law and the Internet: A Framework for Electronic Commerce*, 2nd ed. (Oxford: Hart Publishing).

Thurlow, W.H. (2001), 'Electronic Contracts in the United States and the European Union: Varying Approaches to the Elimination of Paper and Pen', *Electronic Journal of Comparative Law*, vol. 5, no. 3, available at http://www .ejcl.org/53/art53-1.html (accessed 10 October 2004).

Trooboff, P. (2005), 'Foreign Judgments: International Law', *National Law Journal*, vol. 13, 23 August.

Tyler, M.C. (2004), 'Online Dispute Resolution: Applications and Limitations', research for Enabling Government, Enabling Communities, Brisbane, available at http://www.agimo.gov.au/__data/assets/pdf_file/0017/38222/041107mct.pdf (accessed 19 May 2008).

Tyler, M.C. and Bornstein, J. (2006), 'Accreditation of On line Dispute Resolution Practitioners', *Conflict Resolution Quarterly*, vol. 23, no. 3, pp. 383–404.

UN General Assembly (2005), The UN Convention on the Use of Electronic Communications in International Contracts, Resolution adopted by the General Assembly on the report of the 6th Committee (A/60/515), Agenda Item 79, A/RES/60/21, 9 December 2005.

UN Secretariat (2005), 'Settlement of Commercial Disputes: Preparation of a Model Legislative Provision on Written Form for the Arbitration Agreement, Note by the Secretariat, UN Doc. A/CN.9/WG.II/WP.136, (19 July).

UNCITRAL (UN Commission on International Trade Law) (2007), Explanatory note to the UN Convention on the Use of Electronic Communications in International Contracts, New York, 2007, available at http://www.uncitral.org/pdf/english/texts/electcom/06-57452_Ebook.pdf (accessed 18 April 2007).

Uniform Law Commissioners (n.d.), National Conference of Commissioners on Uniform State Laws – Summary of Uniform Computer Information Transactions Act, available at http://www.nccusl.org/Update/uniformact_summaries/uniformacts-s-ucita.asp (accessed 12 November 2004).

US Dept of Commerce (2005), E-Stats, 11 May, p. 2, available at www.census.gov/eos/www/papers/2003/2003finaltext.pdf (accessed 23 February 2007).

Usha, G. (ed.) (2008), *Cybersquatting and Domain Names* (Hyderabad: Icfai University Press).

Vittet-Philippe, P. (2000), 'B2B E-Commerce: Impact on EU Enterprise Policy – A First Assessment' (European Commission, Enterprise Directorate-General), available at http://www.touchbriefings .com/pdf/977/ecom11.pdf (accessed 20 April 2007).

Wang, F. (2007), 'Domain Names Management and Dispute Resolutions – A Comparative Legal Study in the UK, US and China', paper given at the 2007 BILETA Annual Conference, available at http://www.bileta.ac.uk/Document%20Library/1/Domain%20Names%20Management%20and%20Dispute%20Resolutions%20-%20A%20Comparative%20Legal%20Study%20in%20the%20UK,%20US%20and%20China.pdf (accessed 19 May 2008).

Wei, C.K. and Suling, J.C. (2006), 'United Nations Convention on the Use of Electronic Communications in International Contracts – A New Global Standard', *Singapore Academy of Law Journal*, vol. 18, pp. 116–202.

Williams, M. (2001), 'In Whom We Trust: Group Membership as an Affective Context for Trust Development', *Academic Management Review*, vol. 26, pp. 377–96.

Windham, J.S. (2005), 'Resolution of Internet Disputes: The Seventh Amendment's Right to Civil Jury Trial in a Borderless Marketplace', *Southern Law Journal*, vol. 15, available at http://www. salsb.org/slj/vol-xv/2windham.pdf (accessed 29 November 2006).

WIPO (World Intellectual Property Organization) (n.d.), 'Dispute Resolution for the 21st Century', available at http://www.wipo.int/free publications/en/arbitration/779/wipo_pub_779.pdf (accessed 9 August 2006).

WIPO (World Intellectual Property Organization) (n.d.), 'Guide to WIPO Domain Name Dispute Resolution', available at http://www.wipo.int/freepublications/en/arbitration/892/wipo_pub_892.pdf (accessed 9 August 2006).

Witt, N. (2001), 'Online International Arbitration: Nine Issues Crucial To Its Success', *American Review of International Arbitration*, vol. 12, pp. 441–64.

Woon, W. (1988), 'The Applicability of English Law in Singapore', in Walter Woon (ed.), *The Singapore Legal System* (Singapore: Longman).

Xinhua News Agency (2006), 'Online Transactions to Hit US$125b This Year', 19 July, available at http://www.china.org.cn/english/2006/Jul/175177.htm (accessed 22 April 2007).

Xue, H. (2003), 'Online Dispute Resolution in China: Present Practices and Future Developments', Proceedings of the UNECE Forum on ODR, available at http://www.odr.info/unece2003/pdf/hong.pdf (accessed 3 September 2007).

Xue, H. (2004), 'Online Dispute Resolution for E-Commerce in China: Present Practices and Future Developments', *Hong Kong Law Journal*, vol. 34, pp. 377–99.

Zavaletta, J.A. (2002), 'Using E-Dispute Technology to Facilitate the Resolution of E-contract Disputes: A Modest Proposal', *Journal of Technology Law & Policy*, vol. 7, pp. 2–28.

Zhang, M. (2008), 'To Certify, or Not to Certify: A Comparison of Australia and the US in Achieving National Mediator Certification', *Pepperdine Dispute Resolution Law Journal*, vol. 8, pp. 307–29.

Legislation

Council of the European Union, Directive 2008/.../EC of the European Parliament and of the Council on Certain Aspects of Mediation in Civil and Commercial Matters, Brussels 28 February 2008, 15003/5/07 REV5, available at http://ec.europa.eu/civiljustice/docs/st15003-re05_en07.pdf (accessed 21 May 2008).

Directive 1999/93/EC of the European Parliament and of the Council of 13 December 1999 on a Community Framework for Electronic Signatures (Directive on Electronic Signatures), OJ L 13, 19.1.2000.

Directive 2000/31/EC of the European Parliament and the Council of 8 June 2000 on Certain Legal Aspects of Information Society Services, in Particular Electronic Commerce, in the Internet Market (Directive on Electronic Commerce), OJ L 178/1, 17.7.2000.

Directive 2008/52/EC of the European Parliament and of the Council of 21 May 2008 on certain aspects of mediation in civil and commercial matters (the Mediation Directive), OJ L 136/5, 24.5.2008, available at http://eur-lex.europa.eu/LexUriServ/LexUriServ.do?uri=OJ:L:2008:136:0003:0008:EN:PDF (accessed 25 May 2008).

EC Council Regulation on Jurisdiction and the Recognition and Enforcement of Judgments in Civil and Commercial Matter ('Brussels I

Regulation'), see Council Regulation (EC) No. 44/2001, 22 December 2000, OJ L 13, 16.1.2001, p.1, available at http://europa.eu.int/eur-lex/pri/en/oj/dat/2001/l_012/l_ 01220010116en00010023.pdf (accessed 1 June 2008).

UNCITRAL, The Model Law on Electronic Commerce adopted by the UN Commission on International Trade Law (UNCITRAL), Resolution adopted by the General Assembly on the report of the 6th Committee (A/51/628), Agenda Item 148, A/RES/51/162, 30 January 2007.

UNCITRAL, The Model Law on Electronic Signatures of the UN Commission on International Trade Law, Resolution adopted by the General Assembly, on the report of the 6th Committee (A/56/588 and Corr.1), Agenda Item 16, A/RES/56/80, 24 January 2002.

UNCITRAL, The Model Law on Electronic Signatures with Guide to Enactment 2001, available at http://www.uncitral.org/pdf/english/texts/electcom/ml-elecsig-e.pdf (accessed 15 July 2008).

UNCITRAL, The Model Law on International Commercial Arbitration 2006, UN GAOR, 40th Session., Supp. No. 53, at 81, UN Doc. A/CN.9/XVIII/CRP.4 and Add. 1 (1985). It is equivalent to Article 1(3) of the 1985 UNCITRAL Model Law on International Commercial Arbitration, with amendments as adopted in 2006, available at http://www.uncitral.org/pdf/english/texts/arbitration/ml-arb/07-86998_Ebook.pdf (accessed 21 May 2008).

Index

Made in the USA
Middletown, DE
19 January 2023

22484487R00097